PROGRAMMING

SECRETS

*The Underground System
To Learn ANY Coding Language
Even If You Have Never Written
Code Before*

Tom Schweitzer

COPYRIGHT

ISBN: 9798800498516

Copyright and Permissions

Copyright © 2022+ by Tom Schweitzer, TeachMeTom / netzfrequenz software GmbH - All rights reserved.

Limits of Liability / Disclaimer of Warranty

The authors and publisher of this book and the accompanying materials have used their best efforts in preparing this program. The authors and publisher make no representation or warranties with respect to the accuracy, applicability, fitness, or completeness of the contents of this program. They disclaim any warranties (expressed or implied), merchantability, or fitness for any particular purpose. The authors and publisher shall in no event be held liable for any loss or other damages, including but not limited to special, incidental, consequential, or other damages. As always, the advice of a competent legal, tax, accounting or other professional should be sought. The authors and publisher do not warrant the performance, effectiveness or applicability of any sites listed in this book. All links are for information purposes only and are not warranted for content, accuracy or any other implied or explicit purpose.

This manual contains material protected under International and Federal Copyright Laws and Treaties. Any unauthorized reprint or use of this material is prohibited.

Revision 1.2.2-HC

CONGRATULATIONS!

Congratulations on getting your hands on this book!

You made a really smart decision, and here's why:

You want to learn my unique system to learn ANY programming language - and that's exactly what it is going to do for you. This book you just bought is **my entire framework to learn the basics of programming step by step** in less than a weekend.

Please note:

Included with your book is **free access to a private membership area with exclusive bonus content:**

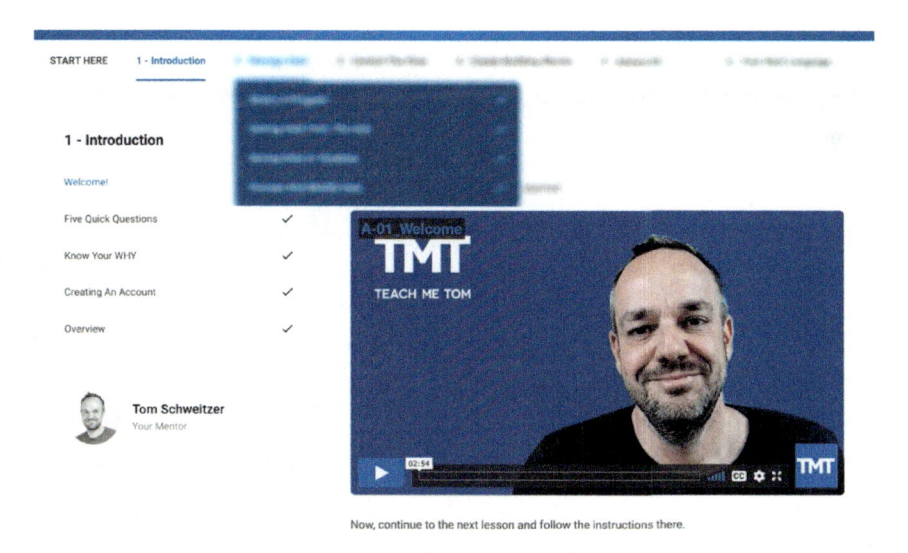

You get free access to detailed video lessons explaining exactly how everything works... and how you can start creating your own programs immediately.

It's my way of ensuring that you can begin coding and implement everything you will learn from the book... right away.

You already paid for this!

Enter this URL now to get access to your free video lessons:

`teachmetom.com/book-bonus`

TABLE OF CONTENTS

COPYRIGHT	**2**
CONGRATULATIONS!	**3**
TABLE OF CONTENTS	**5**
GETTING STARTED	**7**
WELCOME	7
YOUR "WHY"	11
SETUP	15
OVERVIEW	19
STEP 1 – HOW TO MANAGE DATA	**33**
WHAT'S A COMPUTER PROGRAM?	33
INPUT AND OUTPUT	41
STORING DATA IN VARIABLES	51
PROCESSING DATA WITH OPERATORS	59
STEP 2 – HOW TO CONTROL THE FLOW	**67**
IF THIS, THEN THAT ...	67
CREATING A MATH QUIZ	79
HOW TO DO THINGS MORE THAN ONCE	93
EXTENDING OUR MATH QUIZ WITH LOOPS	101
STEP 3 – HOW TO CREATE BUILDING BLOCKS	**109**

DON'T REPEAT YOURSELF	109
DEFINING YOUR NEW BLOCK	117
USING YOUR CUSTOM BLOCK	121
BLOCKS WITH PARAMETERS	125
PLAYING A NUMBER GUESSING GAME	133
PROGRAMMING YOUR NUMBER GUESSING GAME	141
EVEN MORE BLOCKS	**149**
EXTENSIONS	149
BUILD YOUR OWN SIRI / ALEXA	151
BUILD A TRANSLATOR	155
HOW TO LEARN ANY PROGRAMMING LANGUAGE	**157**
AREAS OF SOFTWARE DEVELOPMENT	157
PYTHON	161
JAVASCRIPT	163
JAVA	165
HOW TO SELECT YOUR PROGRAMMING LANGUAGE	167
HOW TO LEARN ANY PROGRAMMING LANGUAGE	169
YOUR NEXT STEP?	**179**
THANK YOU!	**185**
ABOUT THE AUTHOR	**187**

GETTING STARTED

Welcome

Welcome to this book on programming without typing anything "weird" on your keyboard.

I'm happy that you are here.

My name is Tom Schweitzer, and I honor you for making this decision to learn programming.

Believe it or not, this will be easy.

Believe it or not, this will be **easy** - simply because you can't really make any mistakes. There are no "Syntax Errors" you could make (meaning you cannot mistype some strange symbol or word) - simply because there is nothing to type.

We are going to use everyday language, taking it step by step.

It will be fun to experiment, to try out things.

So, here's how we are going to do it:

First of all, before we get into the nitty-gritty stuff, I will explain **how to set up everything you need** in your web browser.

Then, we really get going. Here's how we will structure our journey together:

Step 1

The first step is we learn how to **manage data**.

What do I mean by that?

Think about your smartphone - what kind of data do you have on it? Well, you've got your contacts, emails, photos, website bookmarks...

It's all *data*.

And all that a computer program does is get some data as **input** – like a PIN code that the user enters into an ATM or a photo you take with your smartphone...

Next, the program can **process** the data somehow. For example, after taking a photo, you could modify it by applying a filter to it. That's **data processing**.

And finally, we can get the data **out** of the program again, in some shape or form.

Sometimes it's simply showing a message on the screen, or posting that photo on social media, sending a text message to your messenger group...

So that's what we learn in this first step - learning how to "**manage data**" - input, processing, output. It's the heart and core of every computer program.

Step 2

The second step is to learn how to **control the flow** in our program.

This means you can do different things in your program, depending on what kind of data comes in.

Think about an ATM. When you enter the PIN correctly, you will get a different result – hopefully - than when you don't enter the PIN correctly.

Because in the first case, you want the machine to dispense the money.

But in the other case, if the PIN is incorrect, you want to show a message like "PIN wrong," and do NOT spit out the money.

Other times we want to do things more than once - for example, we will allow the user to enter the PIN again if it was wrong on the first try.

So, this is what we mean by "controlling the flow" in a computer program. We will learn how to do different things depending on the state of some data in your program and how to do something multiple times.

Step 3

Finally, **the third step** is to learn about **building blocks** – how every program is built from tiny pieces, from little reusable building blocks.

Every time we create a new program, we don't have to start entirely from scratch. We can build upon what we've done before by making use of our own building blocks that we assemble together to create something new.

So that's the third step.

And this is the simple structure of our system:

Step 1 – How to manage data

Step 2 – How to control the flow in our program

Step 3 – How to create reusable building blocks

And we do all of that without typing a single line of code...

Are you excited?

Again, welcome - and let's dive right in!

Your "Why"

This is an important chapter. Don't skip this!

We will talk about your "WHY," - and I will give you a fun little exercise to complete.

But first, let me tell you about my goal for this book.

I want to dispel some myths. Learning programming doesn't have to be complicated. Let's get rid of these **limiting beliefs** that some people might have. I want to show you that it can actually be easy and fun to learn computer programming.

When you see your own programs running, and when you get that excitement and the rush of seeing the stuff happening as you have programmed it, ...

... my hope is that it gives you **confidence**, that it changes your outlook on what's possible for you, what you can achieve.

I will lead you through the whole experience as your mentor if you allow me to.

I want to invite you to do a little visualizing exercise with me.

Note: I totally understand that doing something like that in a programming book is unusual. But please, give me the benefit of the doubt, and play along. It doesn't take long, maybe five minutes. All you need is some pen and paper and a quiet place where you can focus for a few minutes.

Read the instructions first, and then follow through:

I want to ask you what it means for you to master the art of programming.

Think about it - what would it really mean to you if you would master programming?

What would change in your life?

Would you have a different job?

What would make things better for you? What would you have in your life once you've mastered programming?

What about your loved ones, your family, your friends? How would they see you differently? What would you tell them about your journey?

How would it feel?

Really get into it, think about it, put some thoughts into it. Nobody is judging you. This is just about you.

Think about what would change in your life.

Your personal situation, the job, the family, the hobbies - what will be different?

Now, before you really do this exercise yourself, let me show you some examples of students who have answered these questions:

Emmanuel wrote:

> "To create apps that can help me run my business smoothly, as well as to help others."

Marcella said:

> "My independence to finally be doing something that matters. And I have a passion for creating apps that relate to my hobbies and for my profession, to be

able to buy the perfect home, to take care of my family, to be financially secure and independent, to never worry about anything but enjoying life and what it has to offer."

Nevena posted:

"I'm sitting in a nice garden during a hot summer day with ice-cold lemonade. I have no worries about unpaid bills. My daughter has everything that she needs for a happy childhood.

My husband is smiling, not tired as usual. We have a nice, warm, and lovely home and a nice family car. And when I look at the past, I see our lives struggle, lack of money, hard tiring jobs, constant struggle just for another day. But now we are traveling on holidays, visiting cool places like Egypt, Greece, Italy, Bahamas.

We're simply enjoying every opportunity that life gives us."

Of course, it's different for everybody.

But whatever they may be - it's helpful to picture your reasons, your life after you have mastered programming.

Because thinking about and deciding your "WHY" will compel and pull you forward, especially when things seem harder than expected...

But your WHY shows you a goal - it offers you a reason why you're doing this, why it makes sense to stick to it, why you will push through.

So, here's the exercise:

Take a few minutes for yourself in a place where you won't be disturbed.

Get a pen and paper.

Maybe put on some relaxing music.

Close your eyes, and ask yourself:

- Why am I **dedicated** to mastering programming with this course, here and now?
- What will my life look like after I have mastered it? What will have changed?

Make sure to really get into it. Put some **emotion** in it. See it in front of you as if you've already achieved it.

Feel it.

Then, open your eyes and **write down** what you saw, taking all the time you need.

Make sure to keep that piece of paper in a safe place.

This is optional, but if you want, you can **share it** with other students here (you will be redirected to Facebook):

teachmetom.com/my-why

Make sure to keep that piece of paper in a safe place.

And whenever you feel frustrated in the following days and weeks, take out that piece of paper, take a deep breath and read it! Picture what you wrote, really feel your "WHY" - and then this will give you the strength and courage to continue.

SETUP

So now it's really time to get going.

First, we will create an account in the system that we're going to use to learn programming without typing.

The system is called Scratch.

It's a project by the MIT Institute - a large, prestigious university in the US. Scratch is perfect for us to learn programming because we can't make any mistakes by mistyping weird words and symbols.

It works simply by drag and drop.

◆ ◆ ◆

Note: If you want to watch me do everything described in this chapter step-by-step, go here to access your free bonus video lessons:

`teachmetom.com/book-bonus`

◆ ◆ ◆

First, we need to create a free Scratch account. It's not mandatory, but it allows us to save and share our Scratch projects.

So, go and fire up your web browser. It could be Chrome, Firefox, Microsoft Edge, whatever it is.

Note: Scratch does work on a tablet, but it's easier with a mouse on your computer.

Go to this address:

`scratch.mit.edu`

You will see the Scratch home page similar to this:

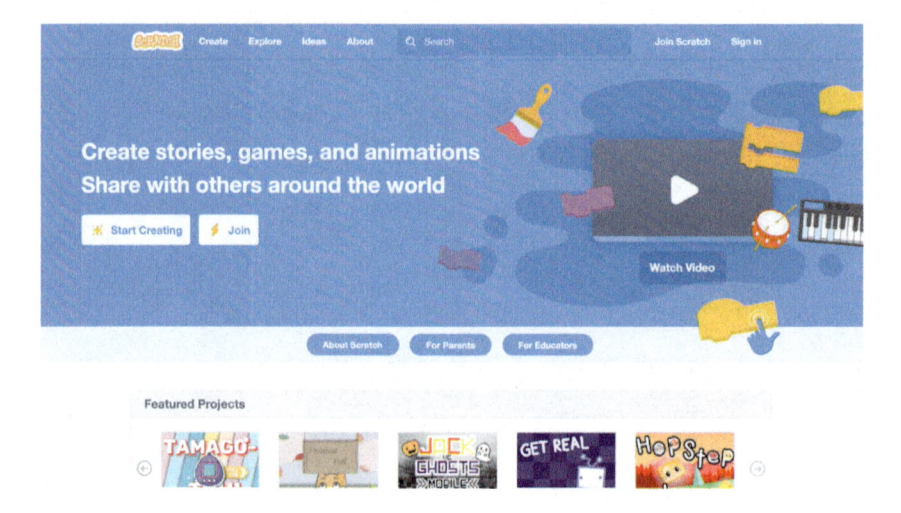

(By the way, regarding the screenshots in this book: Things change all the time on the internet. So if something on your screen does not look exactly like it in the book, don't worry. It will still work.)

Look for a text button "Join Scratch" in the upper right corner. Click that button to begin creating a new account. We need to do this only once.

Next, choose a username. It can be really anything. If the username already exists, just try adding some numbers behind it.

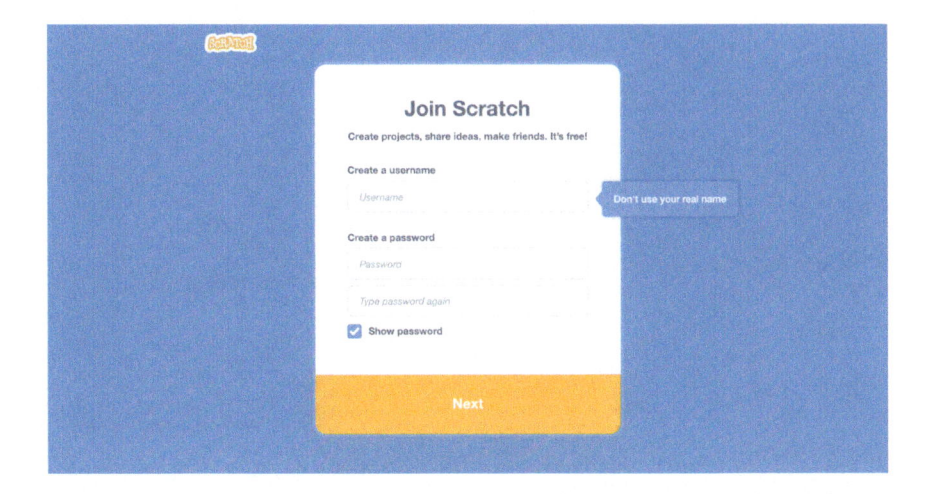

Then, choose a password so that nobody can access your account without your knowledge.

Select the country that you are living in.

You don't really have to answer the next question about your birthyear correctly.

Next, enter your email address. You will receive an email with a confirmation link that you need to click, to verify your account.

Click "Create your account."

You should see a message like "Welcome to Scratch. You're now logged in. You can start exploring and creating projects one to share and comment, click the link on the email we sent to the email."

Click on "Get Started" and voila - you are logged in.

All that's left to do is to confirm your email address - that is needed if you want to share your projects with other people.

The email I received had the subject "Confirm your Scratch account" from "noreply@scratch.mit.edu". Open the email, click on the confirmation link, and we're good to go.

OVERVIEW

IMPORTANT - Before you read any further, make sure to login into the private member area for this book and watch the lesson "Overview".

In the video, I will walk you personally through the contents of this chapter, showing you everything step-by-step, so you can follow along in simple "do as I do"-style.

You already paid for this! Get access to these exclusive bonus lessons for free here:

`teachmetom.com/book-bonus`

◆ ◆ ◆

Now, let us get some feeling of the platform "Scratch" that we are using in our course.

We want to understand what we're dealing with here.

So, if you followed the instructions in the last chapter... (and you are following the instructions and not just reading them, right?) you are now logged in.

At the top is the navigation bar - simply click on "Create" to start a new project. This opens the Scratch editor, and this is where we will be spending most of our time together.

Your screen should look like this:

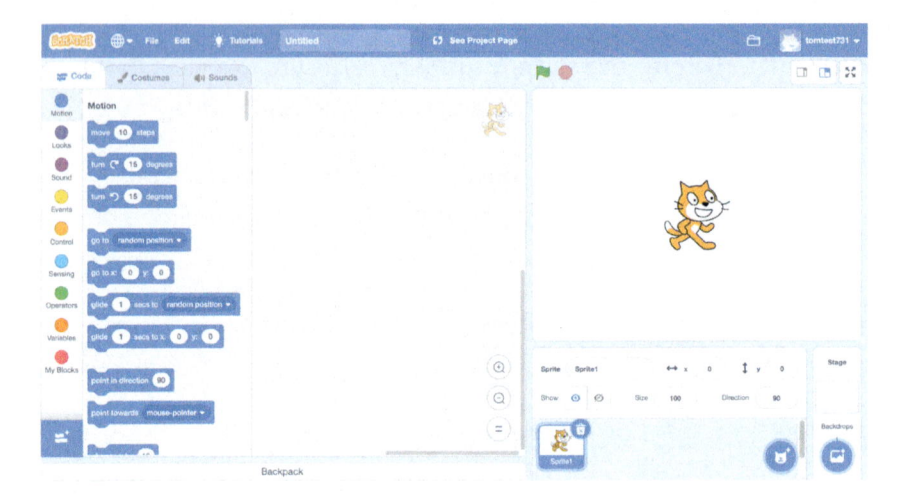

Let's get a feel for Scratch and orientate ourselves to understand what we're gonna be working with.

We've got three significant areas on the screen:

We see a little cat inside a white rectangle on the right, with a green flag button and a red stop button at the top. That area is called the "Stage," and this is where our program will be running - think of it as your program's "computer screen."

The cat is our actor on the stage, and it will be showing the output of our program in speech bubbles.

Left from the stage, you see a big white (almost) empty area in the middle. This is our programming area - we are going to create our program here.

But as promised, we're not going to write our program by typing.

Instead, we will select little blocks from this long list of available blocks on the left and drag-and-drop them one by one to the program area in the middle.

Check out the list of available blocks on the left. They are ordered by their color - the list starts with the blue "Motion" category, and when you scroll down, you will see the purple "Looks" category, followed by the pink "Sound" category, and so on.

You can scroll up and down to find the block you want, or you can jump directly to a category by pressing the colored circle button on the left.

So, enough reading - let's try this out:

Click on the "Events" category, so the list of blocks jumps to the yellow "Events" blocks.

Find the yellow "When the green flag icon clicked" block:

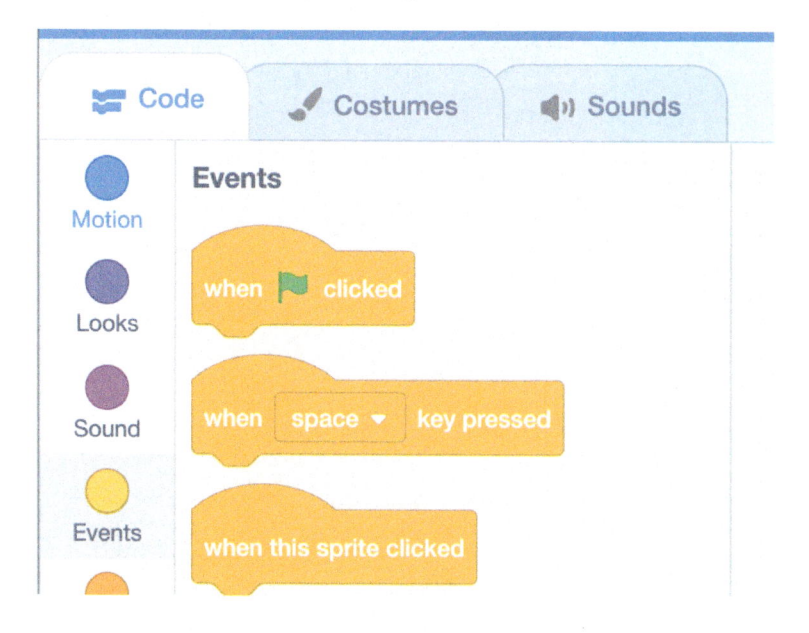

Move your mouse pointer over this block:

[when flag clicked block image]

Press the left mouse button, move the block to the program area to the right, then release the mouse button.

(This is called "drag and drop" - you are probably already familiar with that mouse gesture.)

This is what it should look like:

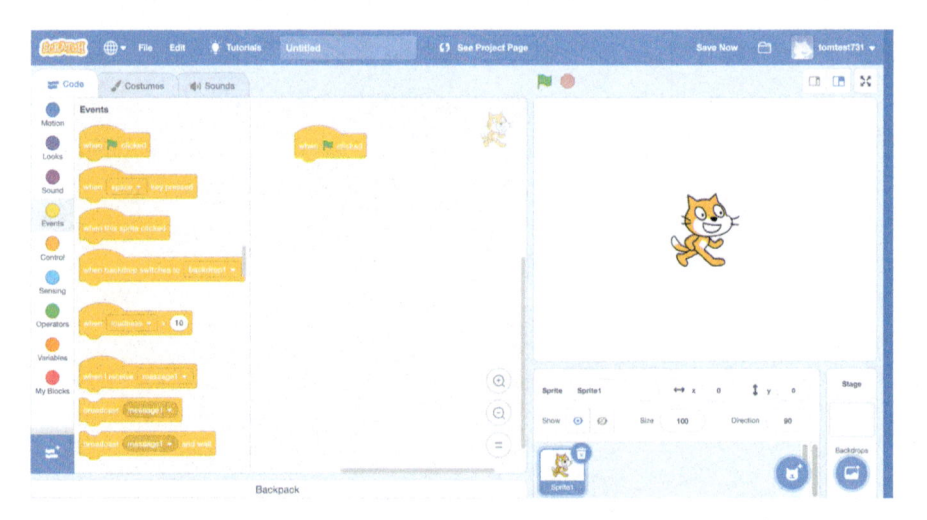

[Scratch interface screenshot]

Easy, right?

So just for fun, let's put another block below the first block.

Find this purple "Say (Hello!) for (2) seconds" block.

You can click on the purple "Looks" category button, or you manually scroll through the list of blocks until you see it:

Getting Started

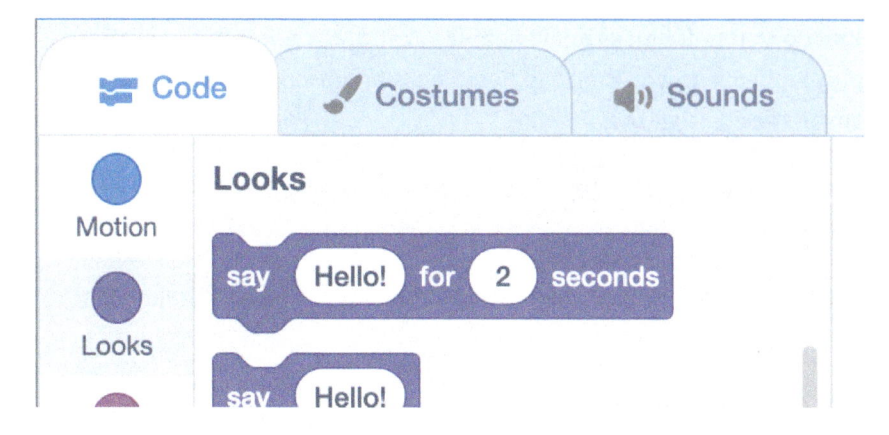

Again, drag and drop it to the right into the programming editor.

Now - take note:

When you drag the "say Hello" block below the yellow "when the green flag is clicked" block,

they show a little gray outline, which means that if you let go of the mouse button now, the two blocks will "snap" together and are connected, like this:

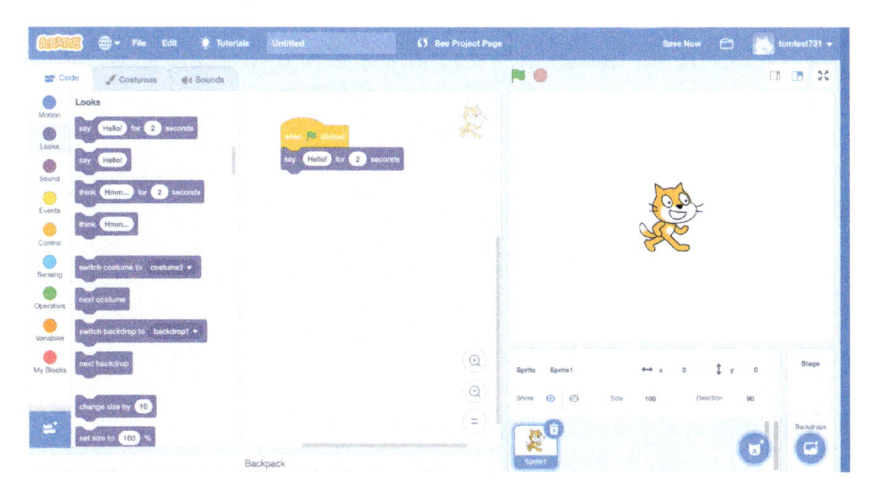

When two blocks are connected, and you are dragging the upper block, the other blocks beneath it move together. That means everything stays connected.

23

How do you pull blocks apart again? - Just drag and drop the lower (purple) block down. Then the two blocks are disconnected and are no longer sticking together.

But we really do want them connected - so, please connect the two blocks again.

So what's with this "Say (Hello) for (2) seconds" block? What does it do?

Well, the words on every block actually tell you what they will be doing.

The "say" block will output the message in the first white bubble for the duration specified in the second white bubble.

Where will the output appear? It will be shown in a little cartoon speech bubble, next to our cat on the stage.

But - no message anywhere to be found. Why isn't there a "Hello" somewhere near this cat, in our output area?

Here is the reason - and this is important to understand:

There is a difference between "programming" and "executing" a computer program.

When we are *programming*, we just write the "recipe" by dragging and dropping these blocks and connecting them...

Think about it - what happens when you write down a recipe for some dish on a piece of paper - let's say, a birthday cake? Of course, the cake won't magically appear just by writing down the recipe, right?

You have to actually *execute* - you have to follow the instructions of each step to create the cake.

So, again, this is important: These are two different things:

Programming is like writing the recipe for what should happen once we run the program, and

Executing is actually running your program.

And - you probably already guessed it...

We can start the execution of our program by **clicking the green flag button** at the top (above the output area with our little cat):

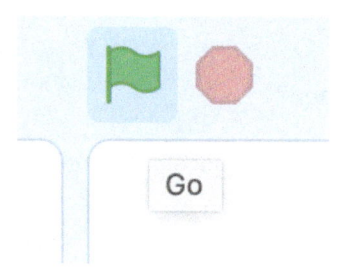

Let's click the green flag.

Now when the program is executing, a few things happen:

- The green flag button is highlighted (it has a darker shape around it)
- We see "Hello" appear next to our cat.
- There's a yellow outline around our program.
- And after 2 seconds, the program execution finishes.

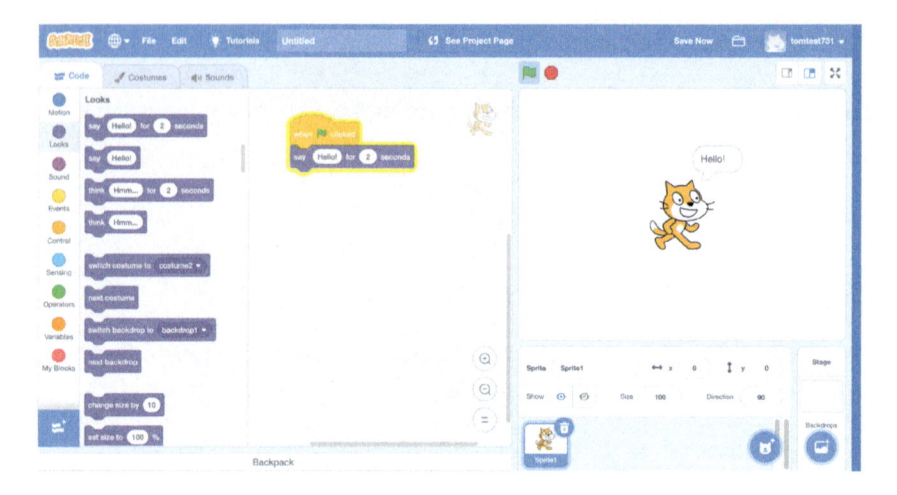

Why do I know it's finished?

The green flag button looks normal again, and the yellow outline around the program disappeared.

So, let's click on the green button again to execute our program a second time.

The program that we have written once can be executed many times - and every time, it will behave exactly the same.

Now, let's modify our program.

To change the duration of how long the message should appear, click into the right white bubble with the number 2 to get a cursor there, and then change the value to 20:

[Scratch blocks: when green flag clicked / say Hello! for 20 seconds]

I just clicked right from the 2 and added a zero. (Make sure you type the digit 0, not the letter O).

To see the effect of this change, click on the green flag again to execute the now modified program - and the "Hello" message will stay for 20 seconds on the screen.

Notice: As long as the program is executing, we see a yellow outline around the blocks.

After 20 seconds, the program stops executing, and the yellow outline disappears. Also, the output is cleared - there is no "Hello" message any longer visible.

So, that's what Scratch is about.

It's really just choosing a block from the long list of available blocks on the left, moving it via drag-and-drop to the editor area, and connecting the new block to the other blocks.

Then, we click the green button to execute the program, and see the execution result in the stage area.

So, what now?

After we have written our first fabulous program, maybe you want to save it, to continue working on it at a later date.

First, let's give our project a name.

At the blue top bar, click on "Untitled" (which is the default title for any new project) and change it to "Hello 20 Seconds", or whatever you want to call it. Hit enter to accept this new project name.

Next, click on "File" - "Save Now."

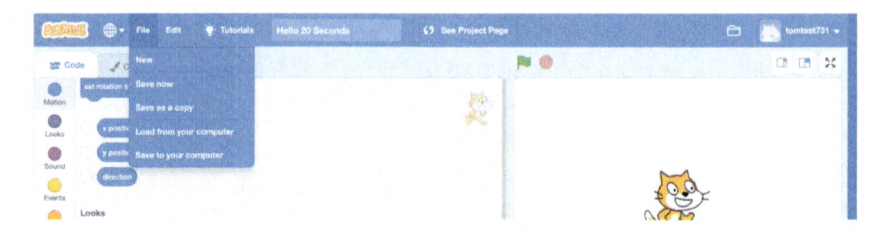

This saves the current state of our project.

To prove it to you, click on your username at the top right, and click "My Stuff."

You will see the project that you just saved:

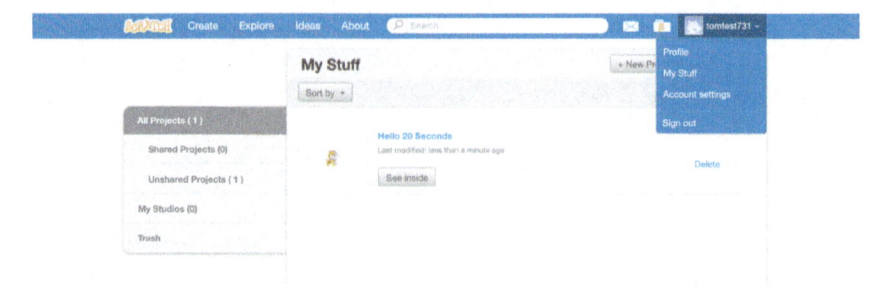

Getting Started

So, if you are returning to this project later, there are two options:

If you want to continue working on the project to modify the program, click the gray "See inside" button (below "Hello 20 Seconds"). This will get you back to the editor.

Or maybe you just want to show your program to somebody else? In that case, you just click the title "Hello 20 Seconds". This will display a page with just the stage area, hiding the blocks making up your program:

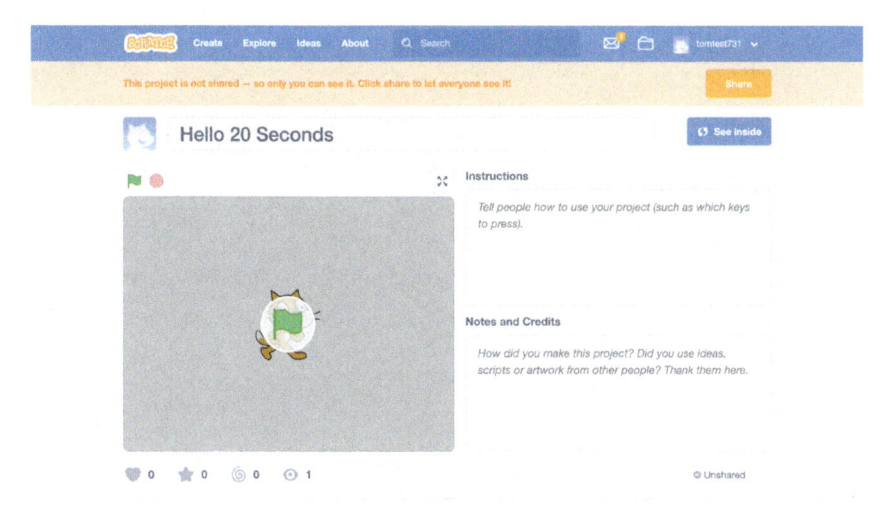

Hit the big green flag button to execute your program without showing its insides.

29

To share the project with somebody else, first click the orange "Share" button at the top right. (Note: This only works if you have previously confirmed your email address.)

Next, click the blue "Copy link" button. You can then paste the link into an email, a social media post, or wherever you want to let the world know about your new fabulous program.

When your friends click this link, they will see this page. They can click the green flag icon to start the program you wrote - and they will be impressed...

◆ ◆ ◆

So, to recap: We have seen

- how easy it is to start up a new project in Scratch,
- how to reopen a project,
- how to share it with somebody.

We have just familiarized ourselves with Scratch.

We're **not** going to cover every block that Scratch offers.

We want to focus on **learning general programming concepts** - so that we can apply what we have learned to other programming languages in the future.

We will do things a little bit differently than in all other Scratch tutorials. We are not going to cover blocks specific to Scratch that will not help us learning about general programming principles.

But trust me, it's going to be fun.

In the next chapter, we are really getting started with the first step - learning how to manage data.

◆ ◆ ◆

Just a requick reminder: If you haven't already done so, click here to get access to your bonus video lessons, where I am walking you step-by-step through everything in this chapter:

teachmetom.com/book-bonus

STEP 1 – HOW TO MANAGE DATA

WHAT'S A COMPUTER PROGRAM?

In the previous chapter, we created our first computer program.

Now, let's talk about the term "computer program" - we mentioned it is **like a recipe.**

Say you want to have a cake, and you don't want to do it yourself. You want somebody else to bake it for you.

It's probably not enough to give them the ingredients and say, "Just make me a cake." - If they've never baked a cake before, they will probably ask you, "I don't know how to make a cake. What do I need to do first? And what's the second step? And the step after that?"

So, you will break it down by giving step-by-step instructions, like:

"Well, first you take 250g of flour and put it in a bowl. Next, you take three eggs, and you break them, and you separate the egg whites and put the yellow stuff into the bowl as well. Third, you add 250g of butter", and so on.

Now, full disclosure - I'm not really a cook (nor do I play one on TV).

But you get the idea:

When you write a recipe, you give **step-by-step instructions** on what needs to be done **in sequential order.**

Oh, and this is important:

The instructions need to be in a language that the person executing the step-by-step instructions can understand.

It could be the world's best cake recipe - but if it's in Spanish, and they only understand German, the recipe will be of no use to them.

Why am I talking about cakes so much? (Well, first of all: Because I like to eat cakes. But more importantly...)

Because it's the same with programming.

A computer program is really just a series of steps that the computer will execute sequentially, step by step, piece by piece, block by block, to create the desired result.

To prove that, let's create our next program.

Put these blocks together:

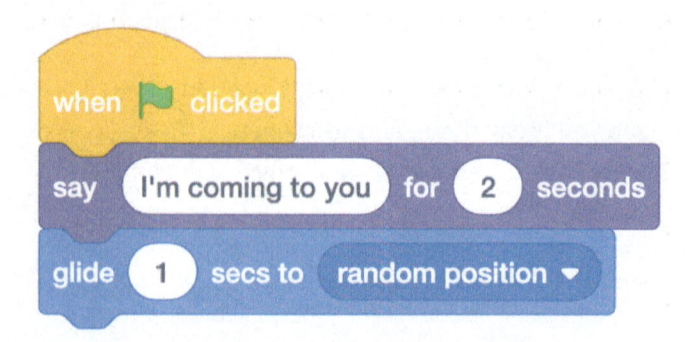

```
when [flag] clicked
say  I'm coming to you  for  2  seconds
glide  1  secs to  random position ▼
```

You will need the yellow "When the green flag is clicked" block to start - you will find it on the left if you click on "Events."

Then click on "Looks," and choose the purple "Say" block, changing the message to "I'm coming to you." (or whatever message you want to appear. Go wild!)

Third, let's try out a new block - click on "Motion" and take the blue "Glide (1) secs to (random position)".

Make sure the blocks are all connected to each other! It will not work if the blocks are separated like this:

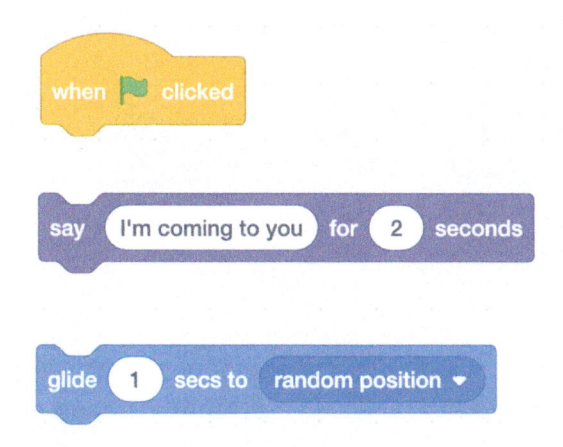

Now, test your program by clicking the green flag button, as before.

You should see the message "I'm coming to you" for 2 seconds, and then our cat will move to... well, a random position on the screen.

Is it working? Cool.

Let's modify our program: Click the little triangle next to "random position," and change it to "mouse-pointer":

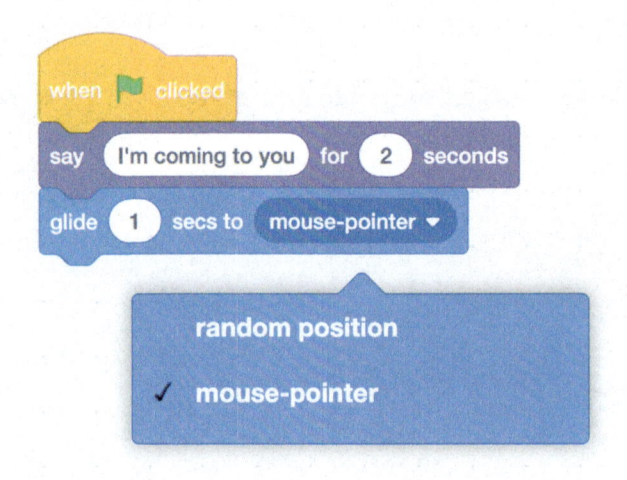

When you run the program now, and you move your mouse pointer inside the white stage area (where the cat Sprite is moving around), you will see that the cat will move in the direction of your mouse pointer.

The critical point is this:

The order of the blocks does matter.

The blocks are executed one after another, from top to bottom:

First, the "say" block.

Then, the "glide" block.

If you change the order, the result will be different. Let's try that out:

Drag a purple "think" block into your program, and put it below the glide block.

Then, set the "think" message to "That was fast!"

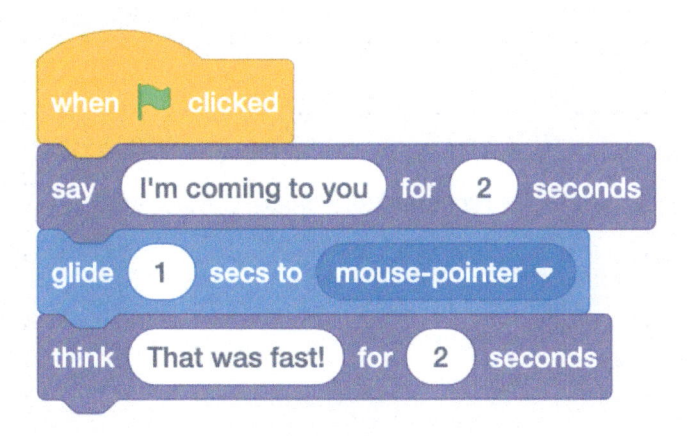

```
when clicked
say  I'm coming to you  for  2  seconds
glide  1  secs to  mouse-pointer
think  That was fast!  for  2  seconds
```

Now run your program by clicking on the green flag button.

Do you see that the blocks are executed in the exact order that we set up in our program?

That's very, very important.

If you think back to our analogy with the cooking recipe - it's pretty much the same:

What happens if you mix up the order of the instructions - like, putting the flour at the very end on top of the cake? Obviously, you would have a very different (and probably inedible) result.

So, to practice some more, let's change the order of the blocks in our program.

To switch the second and the third block, you need to

- disconnect the "think" block by pulling it down, and move it somewhere temporarily out of the way (not connected to another block),
- then disconnect the "glide" block,
- then you can reconnect the "think" block,
- and then finally reconnect the "glide" block.

It reads much more complicated than it is in reality. The end result should look like this:

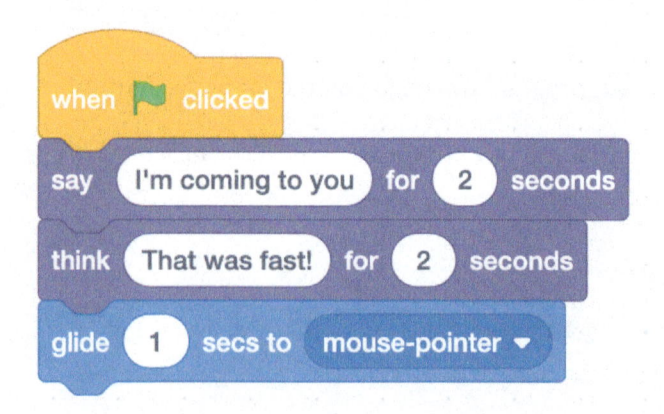

When you run this modified program, you will see a different outcome than before:

1. The message "I'm coming to you",
2. then thinking "That was fast!",
3. and only then the movement to the current mouse position.

So, we proved that the order of the blocks in our programs matters. If you change the order of the blocks, the behavior of your program will be different.

If that all seems pretty obvious to you - congratulations. :-)

◆ ◆ ◆

To recap:

A computer program is a series of instructions executed sequentially, from top to bottom.

When we run the program, the first block will be executed. And only once that instruction is finished the second block will be executed. And so on.

When there are no more instructions to execute, the program ends.

If you change the order of the instructions, you change the program's outcome.

Once we have written the program, we can run it as often as we wish.

Easy, right?

One more thing:

How do you get rid of some blocks in your program - blocks that you don't need any longer?

First, disconnect the blocks from the rest of your program.

And then simply drag-and-drop them into the library of blocks on the left and let go of the mouse button. This removes the blocks from our editor area and thereby our program.

And don't forget, when you're done with your program, you can give it a name in the blue top bar, and then click on "File" - "Save now" to save it into "My Stuff" in your profile.

INPUT AND OUTPUT

Let's make things a bit more interesting.

The two test programs we wrote so far were nice but kind of boring. There was no real interactivity. **Every run of the program was exactly the same.**

Let's change that.

To start, create this new program:

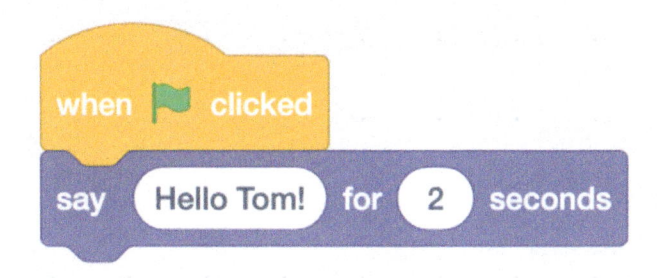

```
when [flag] clicked
say (Hello Tom!) for (2) seconds
```

We have done that before - every time you execute this program, it will say "Hello Tom!".

But what if the user in front of the computer is not called Tom? It is kind of rude to greet them with a wrong name. ;-)

So, let's **ask** the user for their name.

First, we will learn a way to get data into our program (by asking the user), and then we will learn how to use that data later on.

Click on "Sensing" in the blocks library

and find the "ask ( ) and wait" block.

The default question text in the block is already set to "What's your name?" - so just drag-and-drop it into your program, like this:

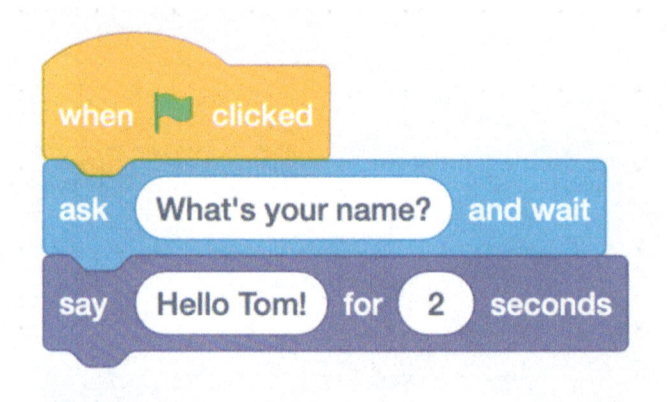

Now, run your program.

You see a speech bubble with "What's your name?" - but it does not disappear by itself (like the "say" block we have used before).

The program waits for user input:

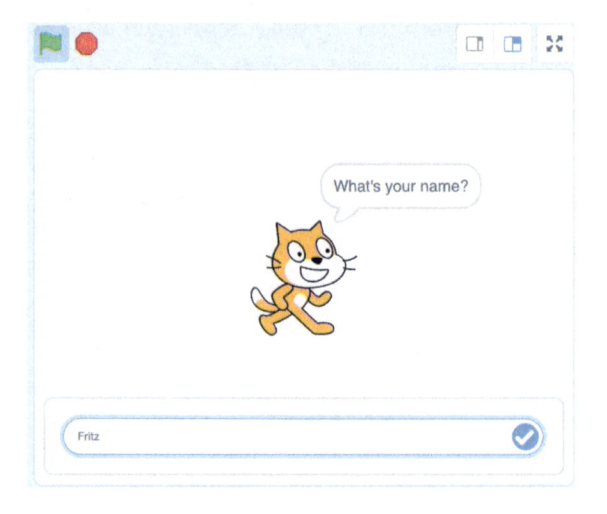

Step 1 – How To Manage Data

Below our cat, we see something new:

a little input box.

If we click inside the box, we can enter text.

Now, please notice - we've got two different roles that we are playing here.

When we write our program in the editor area on the left, we are thinking as the "programmer."

When testing the program in the stage area on the right, we play the role of the "user."

Try it - run the program, enter your name, then click the blue "check"-icon on the right, or simply hit the "Enter" key on the keyboard.

The program continues, but the message that follows still says "Hello Tom" (because that's what the "say" block still defines).

How can we use the answer that the user has given us in the "ask" block?

On the left, notice the little bubble below the "ask" block, titled "answer.":

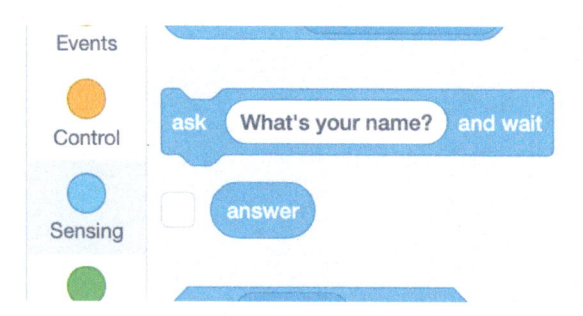

This "answer" shape works like a placeholder. When we run the program, the "answer" shape will contain the user's answer to the previous "ask" block.

43

And its round shape tells you that you can use it in every place that accepts round shapes - like the white message inside the "say" block.

So, take the "answer" shape from the left and drag-and-drop it into the "say" block like this:

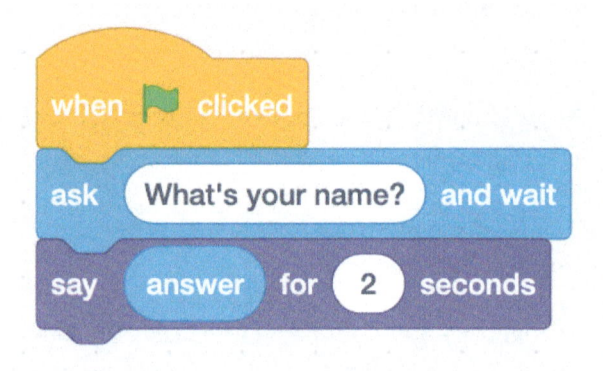

Now, let's run the program again

The user is asked, "What's your name?".

Type your name in the field below and hit "Enter".

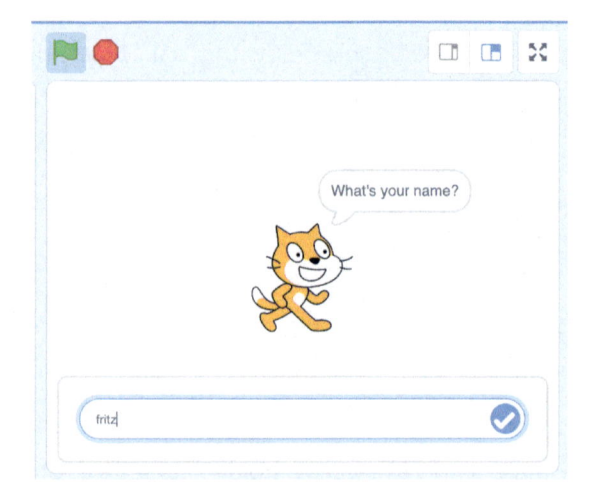

Next, you see the name you entered in the speech bubble:

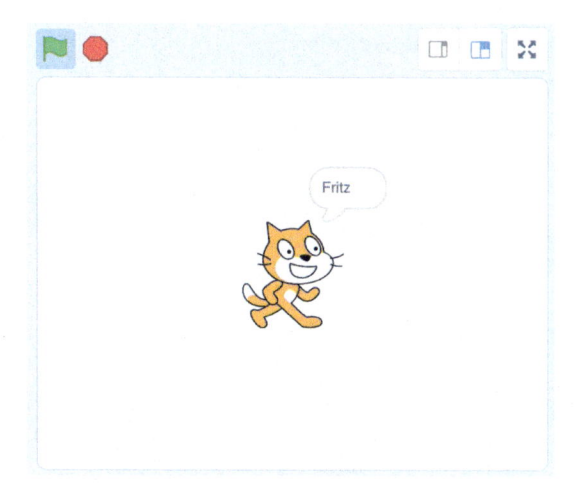

Rerun it, and try a different name.

And a third time, with a third name.

Cool, huh?

But one thing is bothering me - previously, the message said "Hello Tom". By using the "answer"-shape, we have lost the "Hello" part...

Kind of rude again, don't you think?

One trivial solution would be to use an additional say block.

Let's modify your program like this:

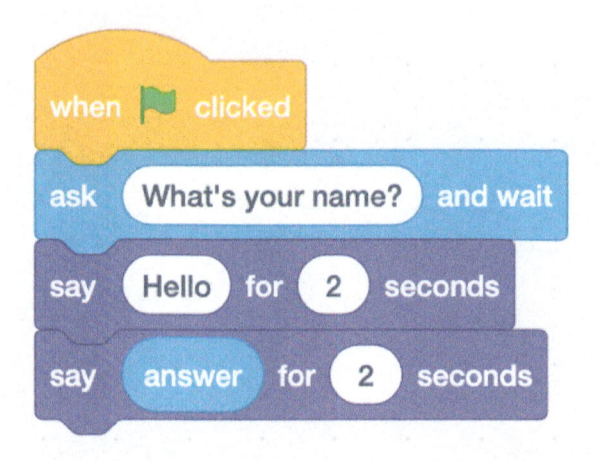

```
when [flag] clicked
ask ( What's your name? ) and wait
say ( Hello ) for ( 2 ) seconds
say ( answer ) for ( 2 ) seconds
```

Run the program.

It works, but it's kind of ugly. What if I want to have "Hello <answer>" in one single message, not separated into two?

The "say" block has just one round shape - so we can either type the message or use the "answer"-shape, but not both.

How can we combine the two parts of the message?

Time to learn something new!

Let's click on the green "Operators" category, and find the "join" operator:

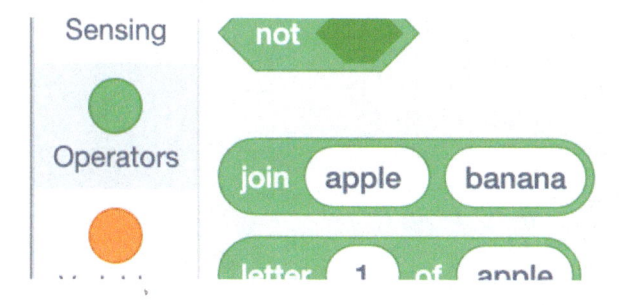

The green "join" operator itself has a round shape - that means we can use it anywhere where we can drag-and-drop a round shape.

This thing combines - or "joins" - the contents of the two white round shapes inside it.

In the example - it will join "apple" and "banana,"" resulting in "applebanana".

So, just for fun, you could drag the "join" operator into the "say" block, and you will get the message "applebanana".

Kind of funny, but what's the point?

Well, we can use this operator to create the message that we want to show to the user.

The first part will be "Hello " (notice the space character after the 'o').

The second part is going to be whatever the user has answered - by using the blue answer shape.

Modify your program to look like this:

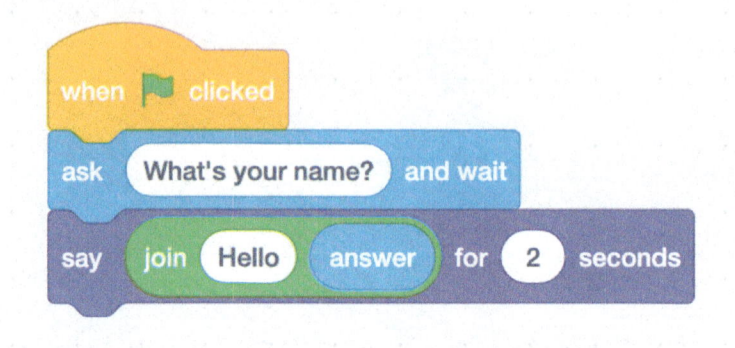

[Scratch blocks: when flag clicked / ask "What's your name?" and wait / say join "Hello " answer for 2 seconds]

So, to be precise:

Inside the "say" message, we have the green "join" operator.

And inside the "join" operator, we have the white "Hello " message on the left (just type into it, as usual) and the blue "answer" shape on the right (just drag it there).

Run your program - and voila:

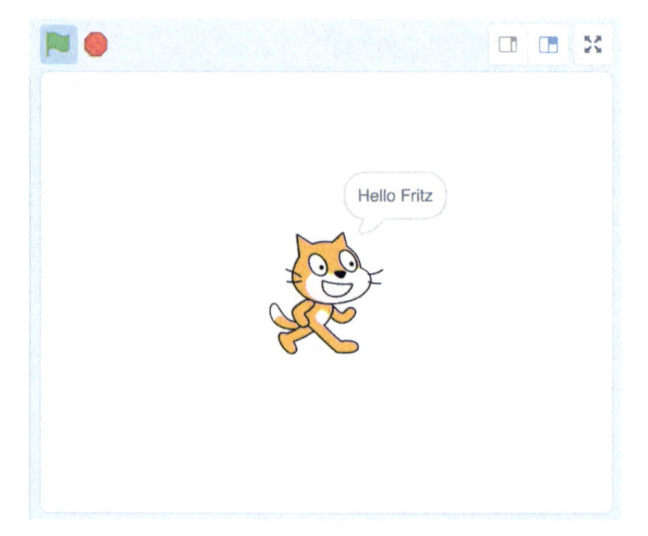

[Scratch stage showing cat saying "Hello Fritz"]

Now, as an exercise, modify your program so that it displays the message "<NAME>, welcome!" instead, like this:

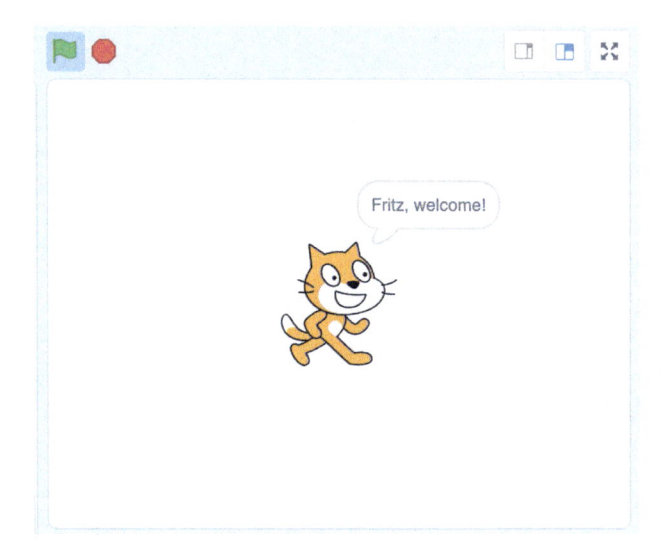

And as an advanced exercise, modify your program to display "Hello <NAME>, welcome."

(Hint: You will need two nested "join"-operators.)

◆ ◆ ◆

To recap:

We have learned how to ask the user for input

and how to use the answer in a "say" block.

And we have seen how to use the green "join" operator.

STORING DATA IN VARIABLES

Let's continue our journey to get data into our program.

This is where we left off:

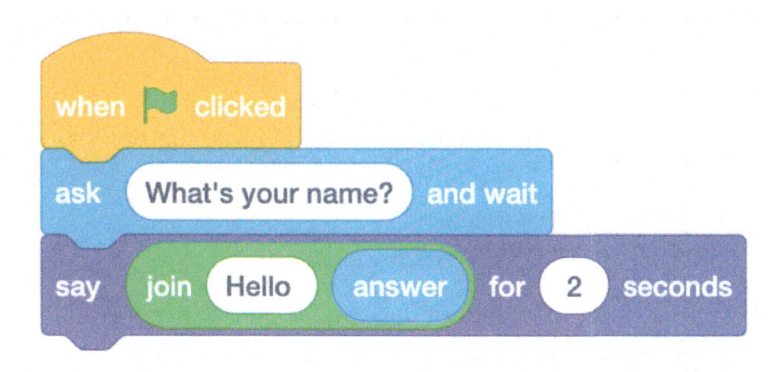

```
when [flag] clicked
ask (What's your name?) and wait
say (join (Hello) (answer)) for (2) seconds
```

Right now, we know we can get the user's name from the "answer" shape that we already used.

But let's see what happens if we use another "ask" block.

Modify your program by placing another "ask" block below and get the user's age, like this:

```
when [flag] clicked
ask (What's your name?) and wait
say (join (Hello) (answer)) for (2) seconds
ask (How old are you (in years)?) and wait
```

The question is: When you put another "say" block to display the user's age (using the "answer" shape, as before) - what happens to the name that the user entered?

This is important:

After the second "ask" block, the user's name will be "forgotten" - meaning it won't be available any longer to our program because the value stored in the "answer" shape always reflects the answer from the latest "ask" block. – By the time the user has entered the age, the user's name will be lost...

What can we do to avoid this?

To "remember" a specific piece of data that we might need at a later date - like the name - we need a place to store that data.

That place to store data is called a "variable."

Before you can use a variable, you have to tell Scratch about it.

Click on the "Variables" icon on the left, then click on the "Make a Variable" button:

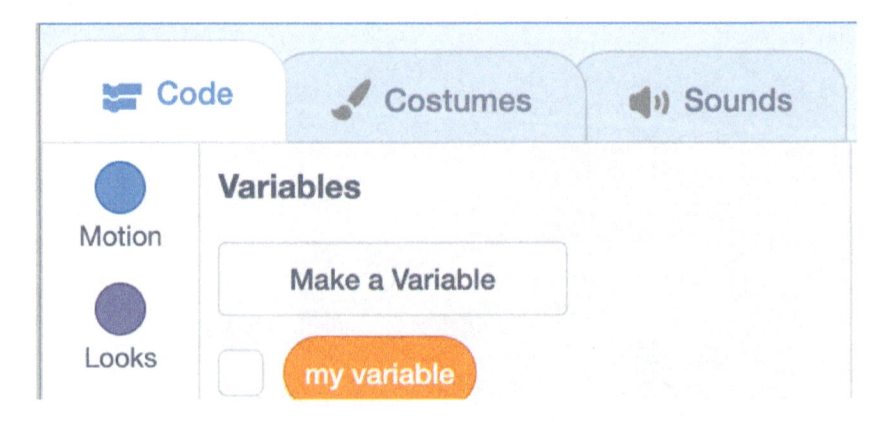

Step 1 – How To Manage Data

This opens up this "New variable" popup window, asking you for a name for this new variable:

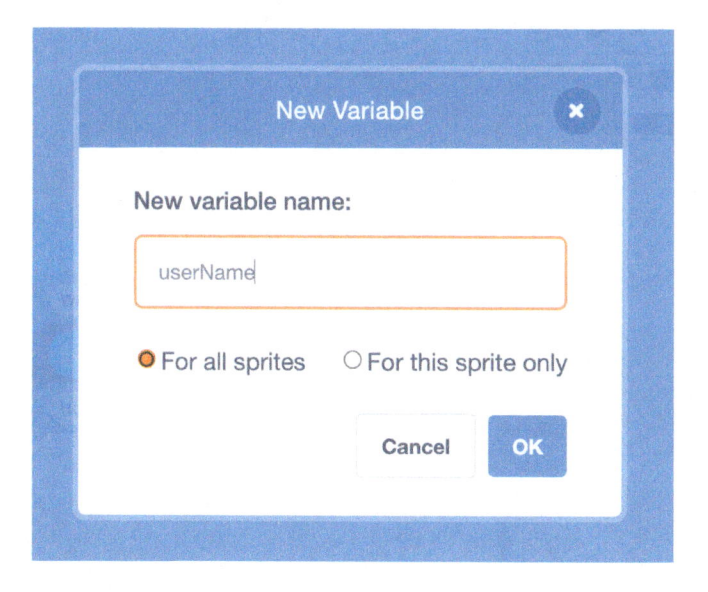

We identify a variable by its name. The name can be really anything, but it tell us what this variable is about (not to confuse ourselves while writing our program).

Since we want to store the user's name, let's call our first variable "username".

(It's not really necessary to use an lowercase 'u' and an uppercase 'N,' but it makes you look like a professional programmer ;-))

Just leave everything else as it is, and click "OK."

Now look what happens on the Stage:

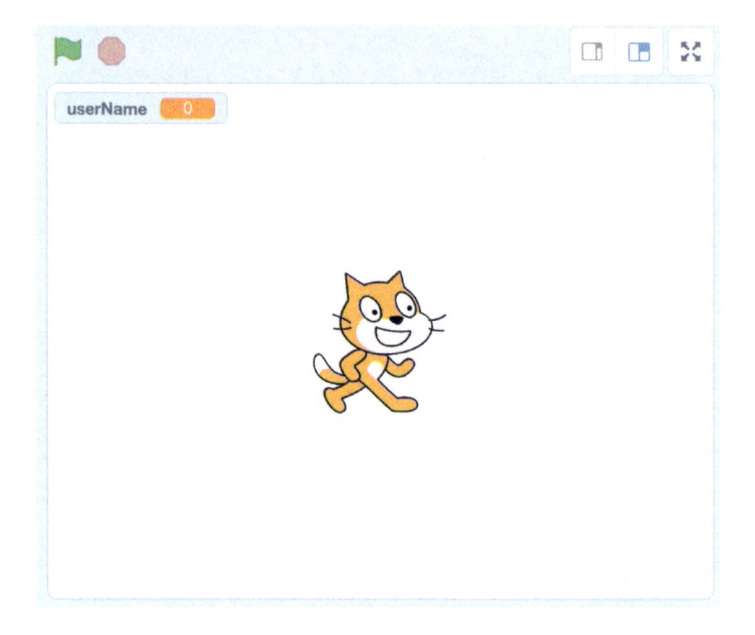

We see a little info box in the stage area. It shows the current value of the variable "userName". (We haven't set it to any value yet, so it's zero.)

Also, look at the blocks on the left side:

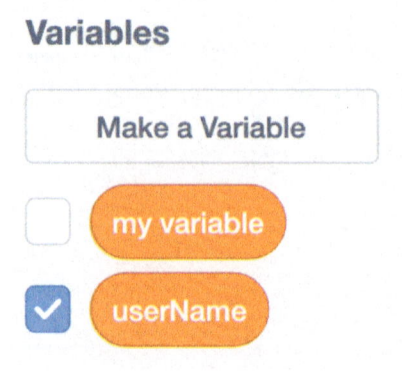

There is now a new round orange shape "userName." (If you click the blue checkbox on the left, you can toggle the display of the little helper box in the stage area on and off.)

Next, find the orange "set [my variable] to (0)" block below the variable.

Click the little triangle pointing down, and select "userName" from the list.

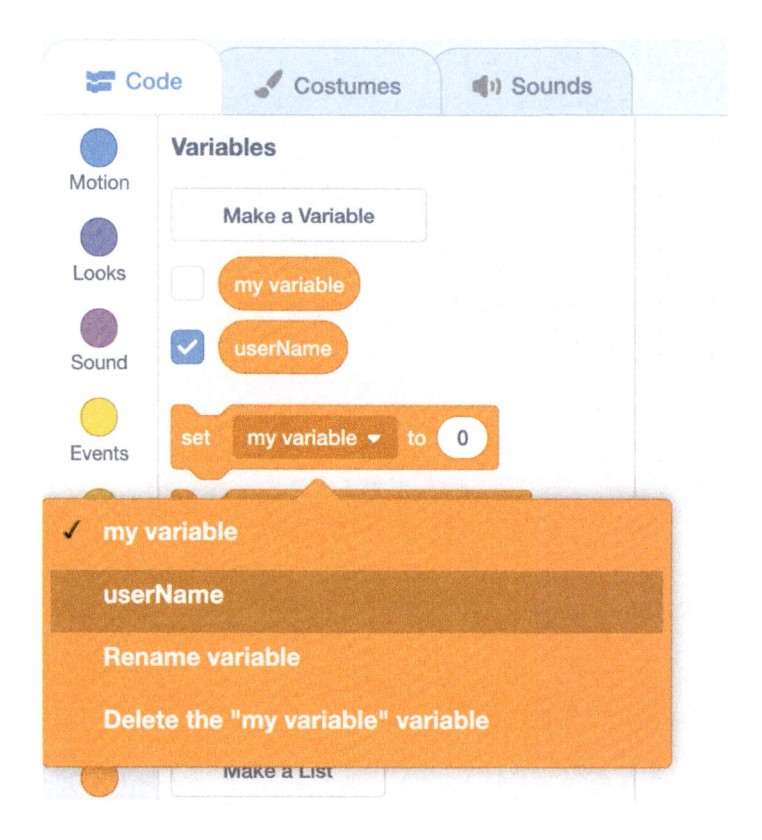

Then, drag this "set [userName] to (0)" block into your editor area, and place it between the "say" block and the second "ask" block.

Finally, drag an (answer) shape into the orange block to replace the number 0.

When you are done, it should look like this:

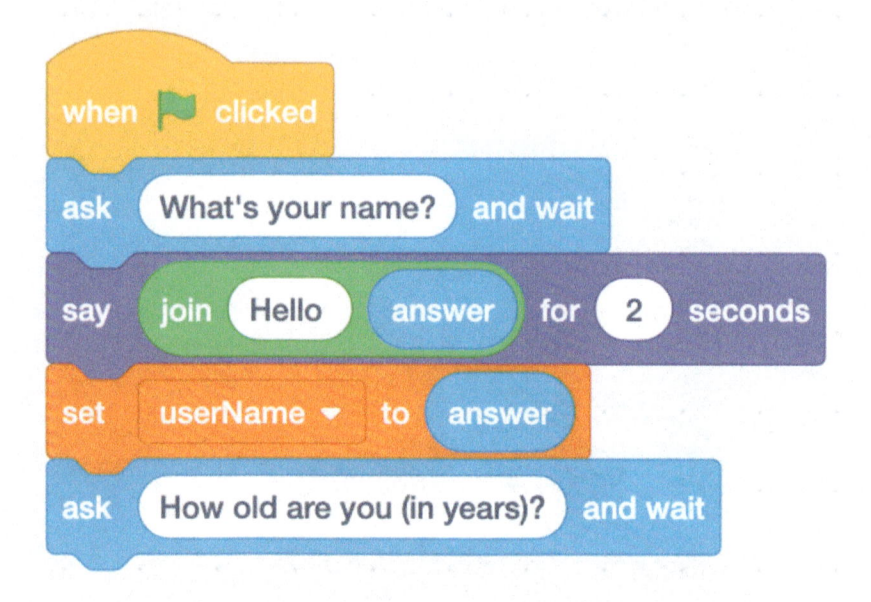

```
when [flag] clicked
ask (What's your name?) and wait
say (join (Hello) (answer)) for (2) seconds
set [userName v] to (answer)
ask (How old are you (in years)?) and wait
```

Run the program, type the name and press Enter

and notice that the variable value at the top has changed to show what you just entered - this is the result of the orange "set" block.

Let's create another variable, called "userAge". (Click on "Make a Variable" again, name it "userAge" and click "OK".)

Now we have two variables - you see both values at the top of the stage.

Next, drag a second orange "set (my variable) to (0)" block, put it below "ask (How old are you...)" block,

and store the answer containing the user's age in the "userAge" variable, like this:

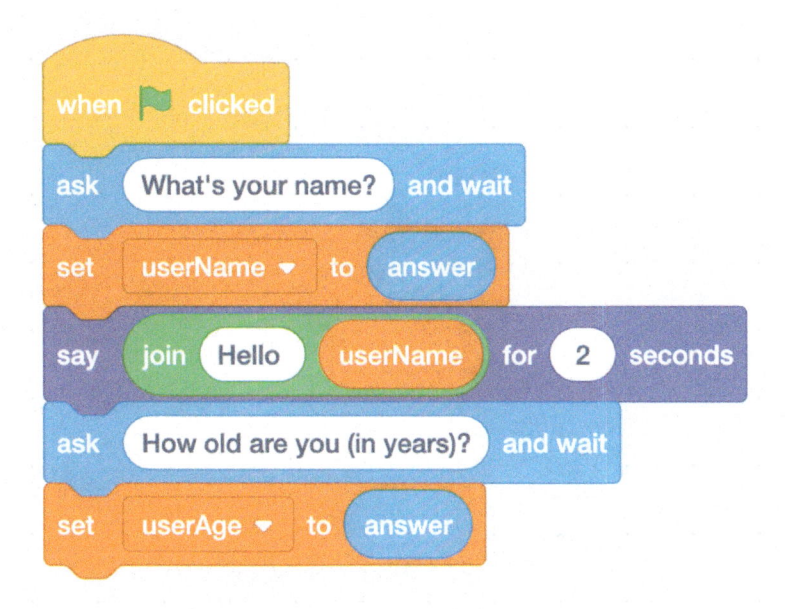

Note: In my program I have also swapped the "say" and "set" blocks at the second and third step, and I'm using the variable "userName" instead of the "answer" shape - but that's just a matter of personal preference.

Run the program and verify that each answer is stored in the related variable.

For example, if I entered "Nina" as the name and "22" as the age, the screen should look like this:

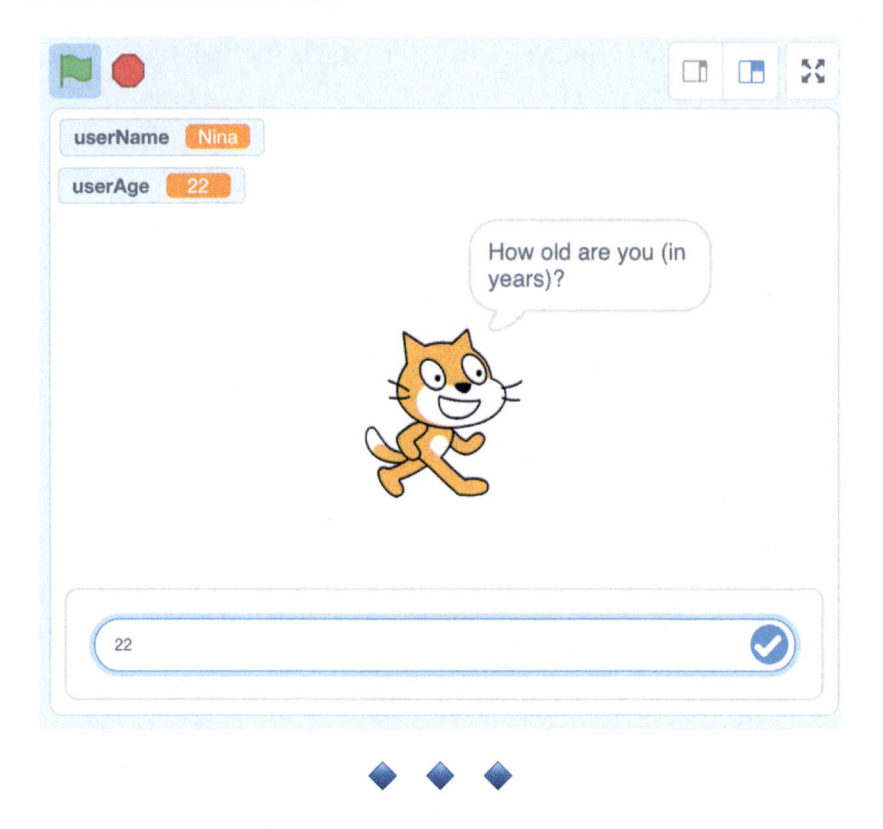

◆ ◆ ◆

So, to recap briefly:

- We've learned that a "variable" is a place in the computer's memory to store data,
- that we need to create ("declare") a new variable before we can use it,
- how to store data into a variable (by using a "set" block),
- and how to check the current value of each variable at the top of the stage area.

Next, let's see how to **process** the data stored in a variable.

PROCESSING DATA WITH OPERATORS

Now it's time to do something with the data stored in a variable - effectively "processing" the data.

Think about your favorite photo app, like Instagram.

You get data into the app by taking a picture.

Then, you want to put a filter on it - you are processing the data that came in; you are modifying it.

Now, our program is a little bit simpler.

After asking the user for their age in years,

let's calculate how many days that equals. That's our simplified "data processing" step.

To make it easy for ourselves, we will ignore leap years. We simply take the age in years and multiply it by 365 to get the number of days - easy as that.

On the left, click on the green "Operators" circle:

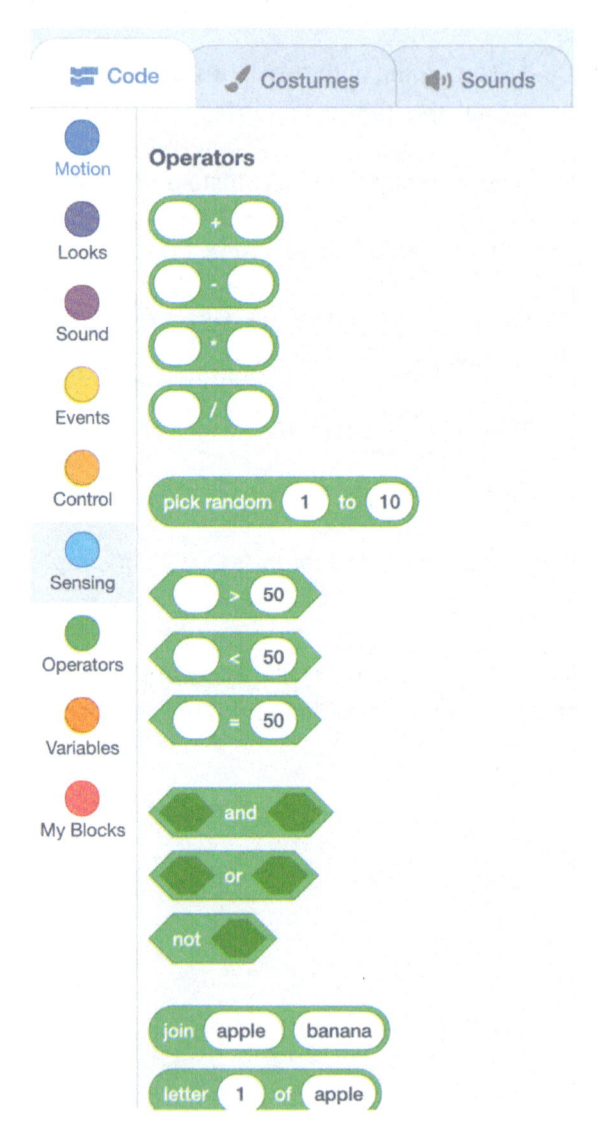

All operators are green, meaning they do their "operation" and return some kind of value.

At the top, we've got four math operators - addition, subtraction, multiplication, and division.

60

Step 1 – How To Manage Data

As we have seen with the "join" operator, each math operator takes two "parameters" (the round white shapes),

does its operation

and then returns the result.

(Ignore the operators with the pointy edges, for now, we are going to use them in the next chapter.)

For our program, we need the multiply operator - it's the third from the top with the little star or asterisk between the two round shapes:

Just drag it into the editor area right now, and drop it where you've got some space. You don't need to connect it to anything yet.

There are two white shapes here (two "parameters") - meaning we can multiply two values with each other.

And - as before - we can drop anything in here that has a round shape.

The first value is going to be our user's age in years. How do we get this? Well, the value is stored in our "userAge" variable.

So click on the "Variables" icon, and drag the orange round shape "userAge" into the first white shape of the green "multiply" operator.

It should look like this:

The second value will not come from a variable - it's just a fixed value of 365 (the number of days in a year).

Click into the second white shape, and enter the number 365 on your keyboard:

So, that's our "data processing" step:

We use the green "multiply" operator to calculate the user's age in days.

And since the result of that operation has a round shape itself, we can use it anywhere where we can use a round shape

...like in a "say" block:

Step 1 – How To Manage Data

Let's test this.

Drag out a "say" block, add it as the last block in your program and drag the multiply operator into it.

Your program should look like this:

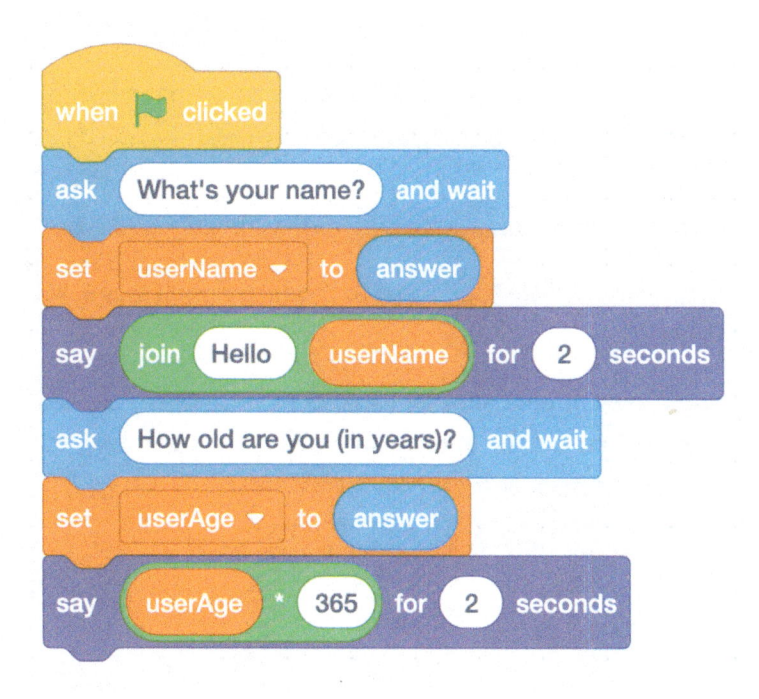

```
when [flag] clicked
ask (What's your name?) and wait
set [userName] to (answer)
say (join (Hello) (userName)) for (2) seconds
ask (How old are you (in years)?) and wait
set [userAge] to (answer)
say ((userAge) * (365)) for (2) seconds
```

Click run and test it.

Does it work?

Great!

Make sure to test it with different input values, including "strange" ones like

- 0
- 1
- 100
- -1

Now, as a next step, instead of simply outputting this number of days, modify the "say" block to output this message:

`"<userName>, you are <age in days> days old. "`

(Hint: You will need 3 "join" operators to produce this message. You got this!)

As a bonus exercise, create another variable to store the calculated number of days, and use this variable in the "say" block, instead of using the green operator directly in the "say" block.

◆ ◆ ◆

That's the end of our first step, how to manage data.

You learned **how to get data in and store it in variables**.

The principle is always the same: In Scratch, we use the "ask" block to get data in, and the "answer" shape in a "set"-block to store the data in a variable.

On a different platform, like a mobile app, the way to enter data could be a touch on a button on the touch screen.

Or it could be a keypress on the ATM machine.

But regardless of the method, there are always ways to get data into your program.

And then, there are ways to **process data.**

We've seen the green "join" operator to combine two parts of a text message. And we've used the "multiply" operator to multiply two numerical values.

Finally, we used two types of blocks to **output data** - the "say" block and the "think" block.

Input, processing, output.

This was easy! So, what's next?

Well, after the first step always follows the second, right?

Let's learn how to control the flow of our program depending on the variable value.

This is what we are going to do in the next chapter.

STEP 2 – HOW TO CONTROL THE FLOW

IF THIS, THEN THAT ...

Congratulations! You have already mastered step one, "How to manage data" - getting data in, processing data, getting data out.

Now it's time to take the next step:

How can we use data to decide what part of our program we want to continue with?

Let me explain what I mean by that.

Let's think about our ATM example - a cash machine.

How does an ATM work?

You usually start the process by inserting your card,

and then it asks you for your PIN number.

So, what's the next step?

Well, it depends on whether you entered the PIN correctly or not, right?

IF the PIN is correct,

THEN the machine spits out your money,

ELSE (in case the PIN is not correct), the program should continue differently... Maybe it displays an error message or asks you to enter the PIN again.

But the important part is that the program does not dispense any money if the PIN code is wrong.

See, unlike a cooking recipe (where step 1 is always followed by step 2, followed by step 3, no matter what),

in a computer program, **we can react differently to specific data values that are coming in.**

We do not always have to execute the same steps in the same order, no matter what.

We can define a **condition** (like "is the PIN code correct?") and execute a particular part of our program (like dispensing the money) only if that condition is evaluated to be true.

So let's recreate this ATM example in Scratch, in a simplified manner, of course:

Create a new Scratch project. (If you are in the editor, select the "File" menu – "New").

As always, start with the yellow "When the green flag is clicked" block (you can find it in the "Events" section of the list of blocks).

Then let's create a variable to store our secret PIN.

Click on the "Variables" icon and then on "Make a variable." Let's name the variable "secretPIN" (it's always good to use names that actually tell you what you want to store in that variable).

Click "OK."

Step 2 – How To Control The Flow

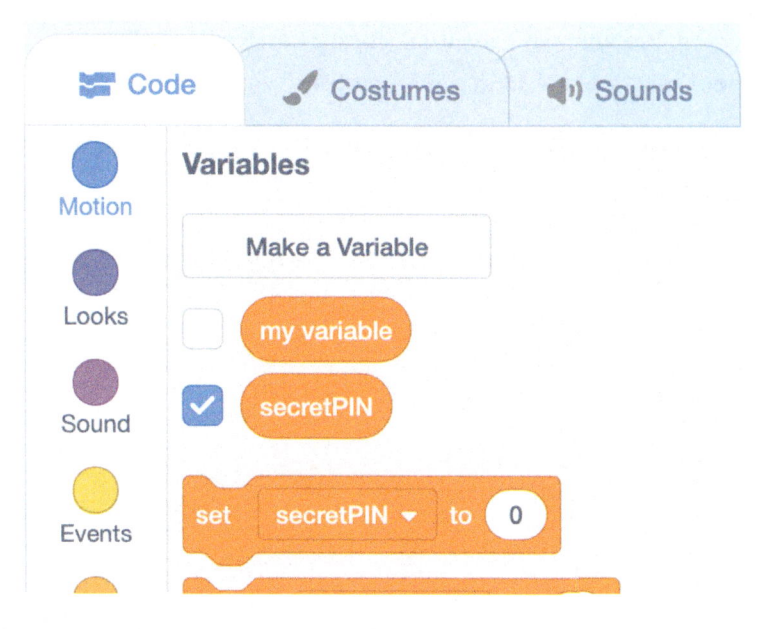

We've got our "secretPIN" variable here.

Now, we could use an "ask" block as before and store the user input in the variable.

But just for now, instead of having to type the PIN code every time we run the program, let's set the variable to a specific fixed value. We haven't really done that before, but it's certainly possible - it makes it easier to test things.

Here's my example:

We said we want to learn how to control the flow, remember?

69

Programming Secrets

In our case: **We want to execute different blocks depending on whether the value stored in the "secretPIN" variable is correct or not.**

So how do we compare the current value of our secretPIN variable with the correct value?

We do this using our little green friends, the operator blocks.

We had seen this list of round-shaped green operators before (when we used the "multiply" operator):

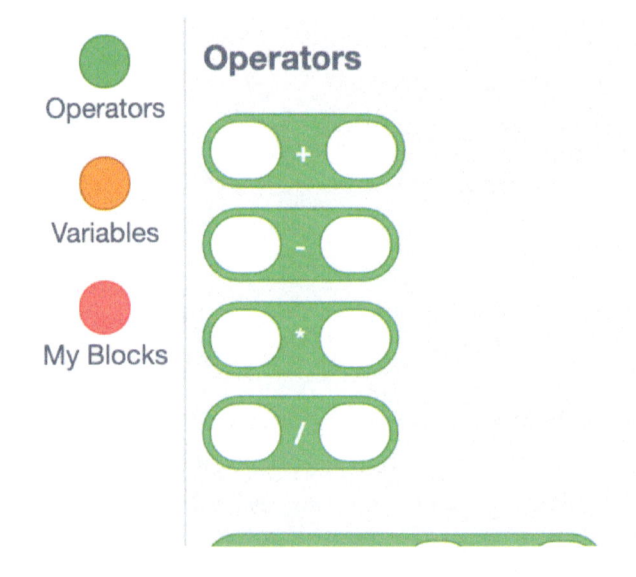

Operators

Variables

My Blocks

Operators

◯ + ◯

◯ - ◯

◯ * ◯

◯ / ◯

Step 2 – How To Control The Flow

You need to scroll down a bit until you see the **comparison operators** - you recognize them by their sharp pointy edges:

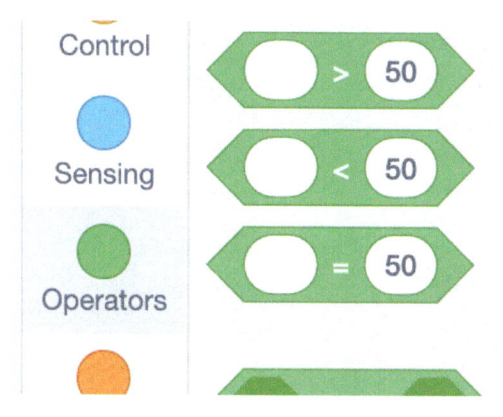

We have not used them before. These operators simply compare two values with each other, and the result of this comparison is either *true* or *false*.

(We will see what this means shortly).

The first comparison operator checks whether the value on the left is greater than the value on the right.

The second one checks whether the left is smaller than the right.

And the third is the one that we need - it checks for equality.

Drag this "equals" operator somewhere into your editor area, but don't attach it to anything yet.

In our case, we want to compare the value of our secretPIN variable with the correct pin (in our example, it's just some made up combination, like 1234).

Click on "Variables" again and drag the "secretPIN" round shape into the first white round shape.

Let's assume that the correct value is 1234, so click into the second white round shape, and type 1234 and hit enter.

It should look like this:

`secretPIN = 1234`

This block compares the value of the "secretPIN" variable with "1234".

Now, this is important:

The result of any comparison can only be *true* or *false*.

There's no in-between.

If the secretPIN actually is "1234," - then the comparison result is *true*.

If the secretPIN's value is anything else, like "9999," - then it's not equal to "1234", and the comparison result is *false*.

(In programming, this is called a "boolean" data type. There are other data types like text or numerical data types, but we do not need to worry about them right now.)

Now that we have created our comparison with that pointy edges, we need a place to put it to use.

Step 2 – How To Control The Flow

Click on "Control," then scroll down until you see this "If then" block:

Drag this block it into the editor area, and attach it to the "set" block.

Note that this block has a shape inside that takes a pointy comparison operator, like the one that we have just prepared.

So, let's drag your green comparison into the "if then" block, like that:

Note: If you are having problems, make sure your mouse pointer is directly above the green operator, not the orange "secretPIN" shape (or you would drag the "secretPIN" out of the comparison operator again - which is not what we want).

Congratulations, you have just created an "if then statement".

IF the condition inside is *true*, THEN it will execute the blocks in between the brackets.

(Currently, there are none, but we will put something into the brackets in a moment.)

If the condition is *false*, then the whole "If Then" block is skipped - the blocks inside the brackets won't get executed, and the program execution continues with the next block after the "if then block".

So, let's try that out:

Put a "say" block inside the "if then" block, saying "PIN correct!".

And add another "say" block after the "if then" block, saying "The end.".

Your program should look like this:

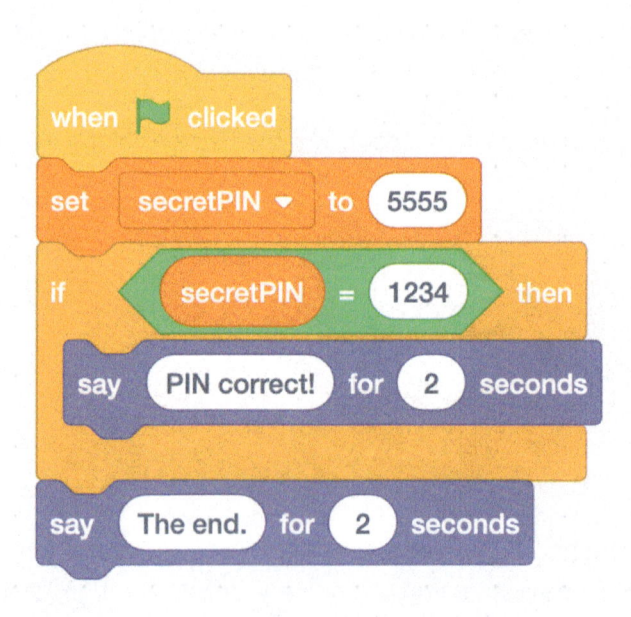

```
when ⚑ clicked
set secretPIN ▼ to 5555
if  secretPIN = 1234  then
    say PIN correct! for 2 seconds
say The end. for 2 seconds
```

Ensure that you are dragging the "say PIN correct!" block inside the "if" bracket - not above it, not below it, but inside. Everything you put inside will only be executed if the green condition is *true*.

So, let's try this out. Run your program.

What happens?

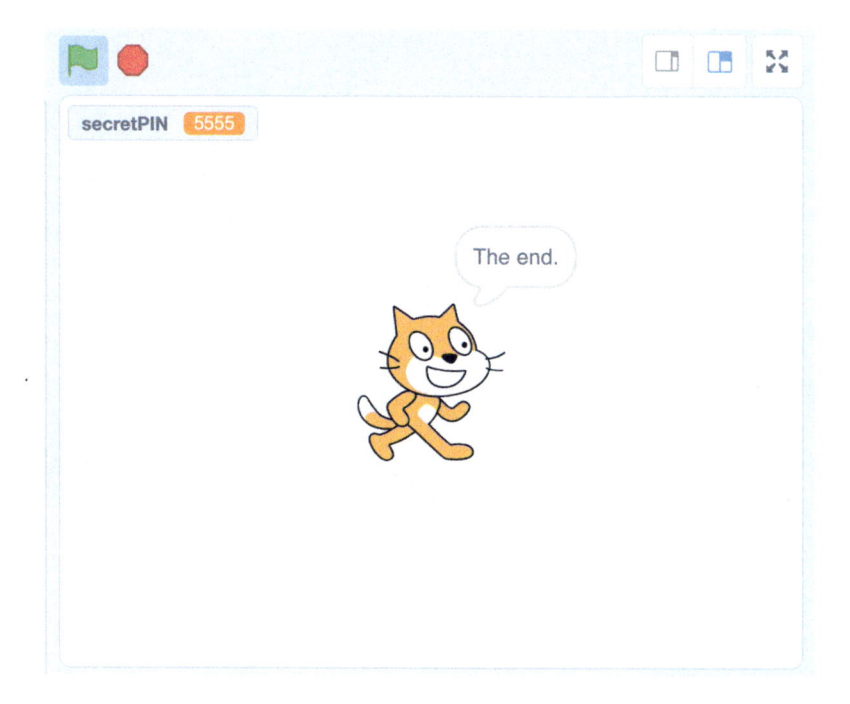

[Scratch stage showing: secretPIN 5555 at top, cat sprite saying "The end."]

First of all, you see at the top that the "secretPIN" value is indeed set to 5555.

Next, notice that you only see the "The end." message.

Why is that?

Well, because the result of the comparison "secretPIN = 1234" is *false*, that's why.

Because the comparison result is *false*, the "say" block inside the if bracket will not get executed. The program continues with the next block after the "if" bracket (which happens to be the "say (The end.)" block.

You can execute the current program as many times as you want - you will never see the "PIN correct!" message.

75

Now, let's set the secretPIN variable to the correct value of 1234, and run the modified program:

`set secretPIN to 1234`

Now you see "PIN correct" first, and then "The end."

Are you getting this?

With the "if then" block, we have a way to react differently depending on what the values of some variable is.

What happens if the condition is *false* and we want to execute a different part of our code ONLY if the condition is *false*?

We can use the "extended" version of this block, the "if then else" block. You can find it under "Control", directly below the "if then" block.

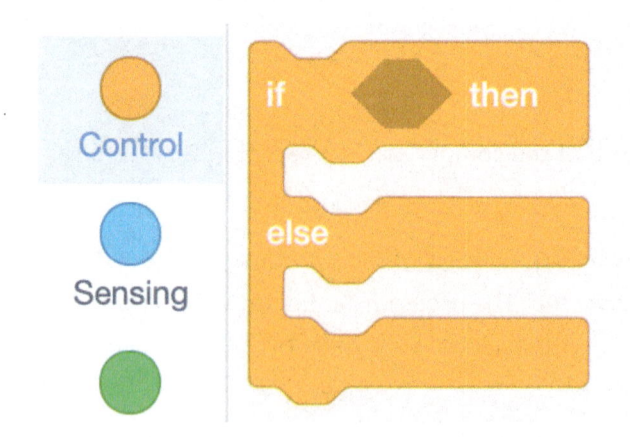

You can probably tell where this is going, right?

76

Step 2 – How To Control The Flow

The first (upper) bracket contains the blocks that will be executed only if the condition is *true*, and the second (lower) bracket contains the blocks that will be executed only if the condition is *false*.

So, let's try this:

Replace the "if then" block with the "if then else" block, and put a "say" block in each bracket, like this:the "if then" block with the "if then else" block, and put a "say" block in each bracket, like this:

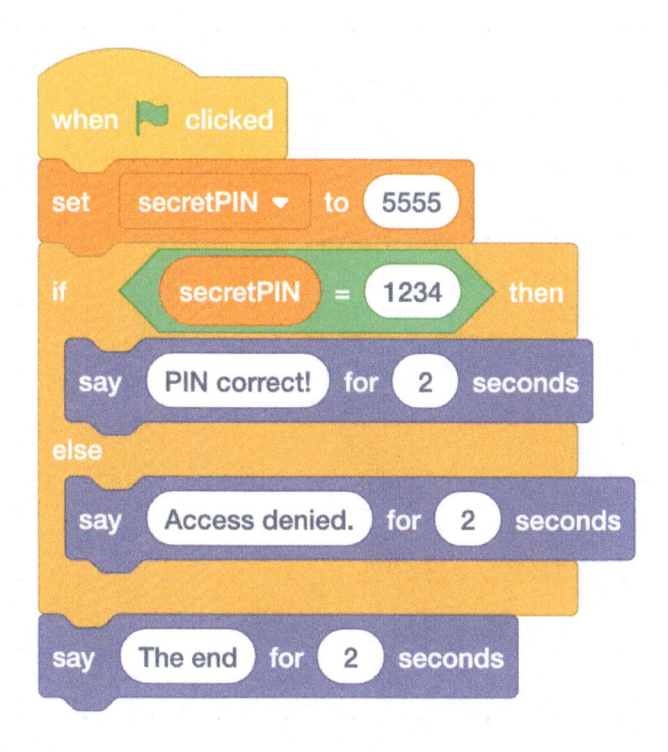

```
when [flag] clicked
set secretPIN ▼ to 5555
if <secretPIN = 1234> then
    say PIN correct! for 2 seconds
else
    say Access denied. for 2 seconds

say The end for 2 seconds
```

Make sure to test this for different values of "secretPIN".

Try the 'positive' case (1234), and a couple of negative cases (like 5555).

You should either see the "PIN correct!" message or the "Access denied." message - but never both!

77

As an exercise, you can add an "ask" block at the top, to let users enter their PIN code. (You then need to replace the hardcoded 5555 value in the "set" block code with the (answer) shape.)

◆ ◆ ◆

In the next chapter, let's expand on that "if then else" concept.

CREATING A MATH QUIZ

Now let's do something different.

Let's create a little game, and I'm going to show you the result first - how the program looks and works from the user's perspective.

And then, we talk about how to write a program to achieve this result.

So, when I run the program, I see a simple math exercise I need to solve - a simple addition of two random integer (whole) numbers (the messages are shown one by one):

Next, I am asked for the result of that addition:

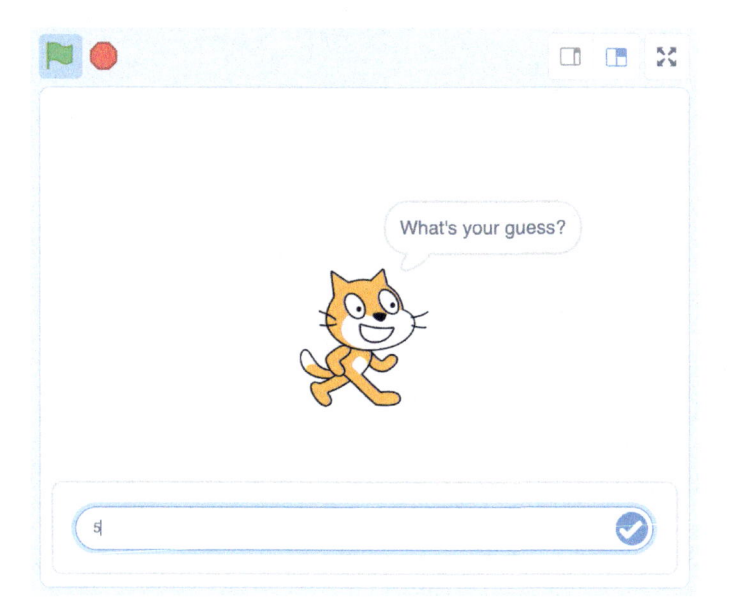

Well, 3 + 2 equals 5,

so I type in 5 and hit enter.

If I have entered the correct result, I am shown this message:

> Yes, that's correct!

And the program ends.

Otherwise (in case the number I gave was not correct), I am shown this message instead:

> Sorry, the correct answer is: 5

And the program ends.

That is the whole program. Okay, so how will we implement that?

Let's break it down:

Step 2 – How To Control The Flow

As with the ATM and PIN example before, the output of the program ("Yes, that's correct" or "Sorry, the correct answer is: X") depends on the user's input.

There is a condition involved:

If the user gets the result right,

then we will show a success message,

else we will show a different message (with the correct result).

So, first let's think about what kind of variables we need.

The two numbers should be chosen at random with each execution (we will learn how to do that soon),

so we need variables for the two numbers - let's call them "num1" and "num2".

We also want a variable to store the result, called "correctResult",

and finally a variable to store the user's input, called "userGuess."

81

So, let's create all the variables:

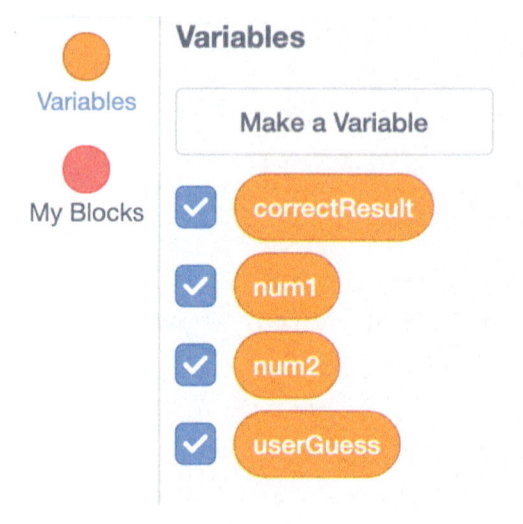

(Don't worry about the "my variable" not showing in the screenshot.)

Next, it's always a good idea to break the task down into simpler sub-tasks.

We do not try to implement everything at once.

We always want to start our program using the "When the green flag is clicked" block, so let's get that from the "Events" category.

Next, let's set the variable values for the math exercise - the values of the "num1", "num2" and "correctResult" variables.

Similar to the ATM example, we set "num1" and "num2" to static values.

(In the end, we will choose the values for "num1" and "num2" at random - but just for now, it's easier to test with static, known numbers.)

So, set "num1" to 2,

set "num2" to 3,

Step 2 – How To Control The Flow

and set "correctResult" to the addition of num1 + num2. (You will need the green "addition" operator.)

When you have done that, your program should look like this:

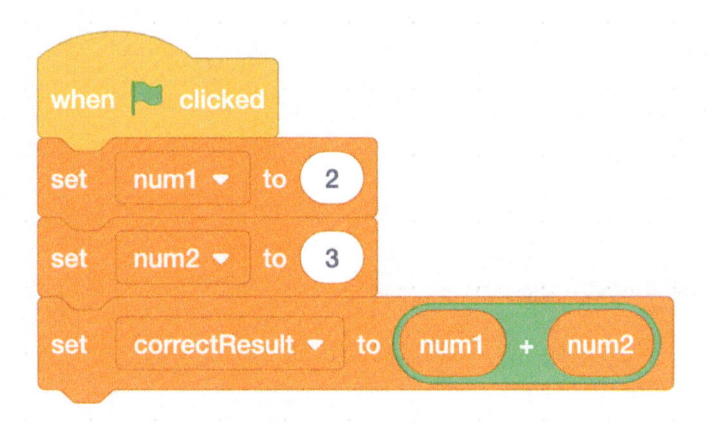

```
when [flag] clicked
set num1 ▼ to 2
set num2 ▼ to 3
set correctResult ▼ to ( num1 + num2 )
```

If you click on "Run," you can verify that the values have been set correctly:

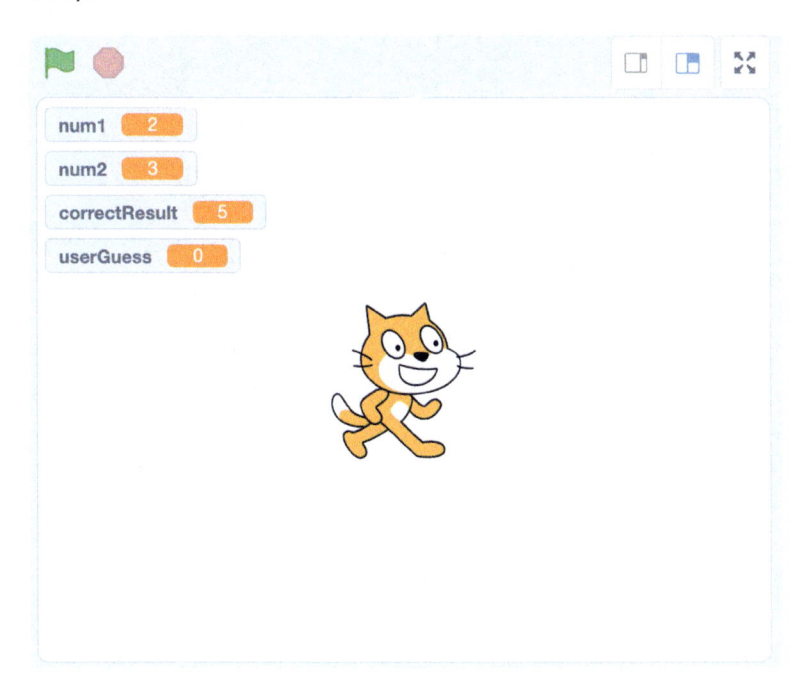

num1 2
num2 3
correctResult 5
userGuess 0

83

Meaning, "num1" has been set to 2,

"num2" is set to 3",

and "correctResult" is 5 (which is the sum of 2 plus 3)

- that works.

(We haven't set "userGuess" so far, that's why it still has the initial value of 0.)

Let's continue with the next part:

Showing the user the math exercise they need to solve:

You can simply use three "say" blocks one after another.

(Note: Make sure to use the "num1" and "num2" variables instead of the numbers "3" and "2" in the "say" blocks.)

Step 2 – How To Control The Flow

When you are done, your program should look like this:

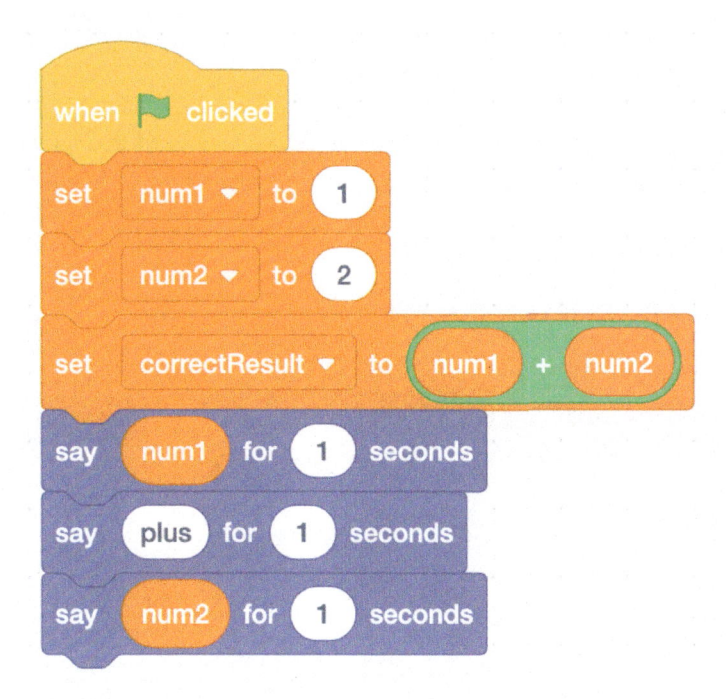

```
when [flag] clicked
set num1 to 1
set num2 to 2
set correctResult to num1 + num2
say num1 for 1 seconds
say plus for 1 seconds
say num2 for 1 seconds
```

If you want, you could combine everything together into a single "say" block instead:

(To improve readability, make sure to type a space before and after "plus".)

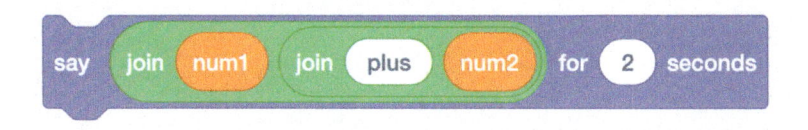

```
say join num1 join plus num2 for 2 seconds
```

Hit run and test that everything works as expected so far.

What's the next sub-problem?

Well, we have shown the user the exercise - now it's time to ask them for their guess.

Click on "Sensing" and attach an "ask" block at the end of your program, and modify the question to be "What's your guess?".

Next, store the user's (answer) into the variable "userGuess".

Here's what it should look like:

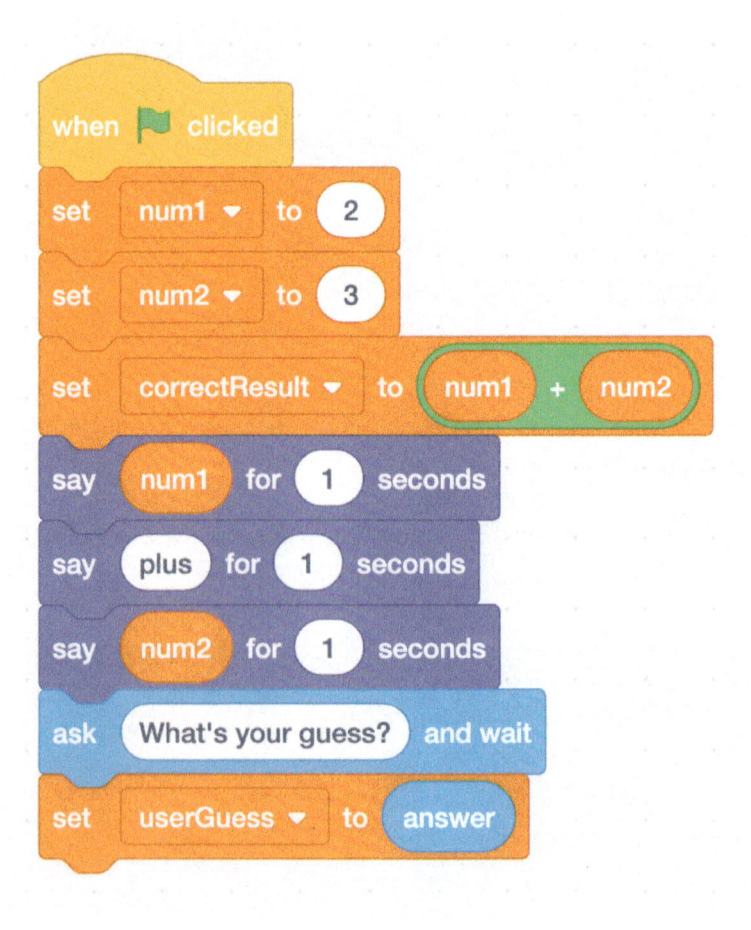

```
when [flag] clicked
set num1 to 2
set num2 to 3
set correctResult to (num1 + num2)
say num1 for 1 seconds
say plus for 1 seconds
say num2 for 1 seconds
ask What's your guess? and wait
set userGuess to answer
```

Again, let's test this.

You see - **we test early, and we test often**. Every time we add some functionality, we can test it to ensure our program still behaves correctly.

Hit run, wait for the "say" blocks to show the exercise and then enter your guess.

Verify at the top that the "userGuess" variable has been set to what you just entered:

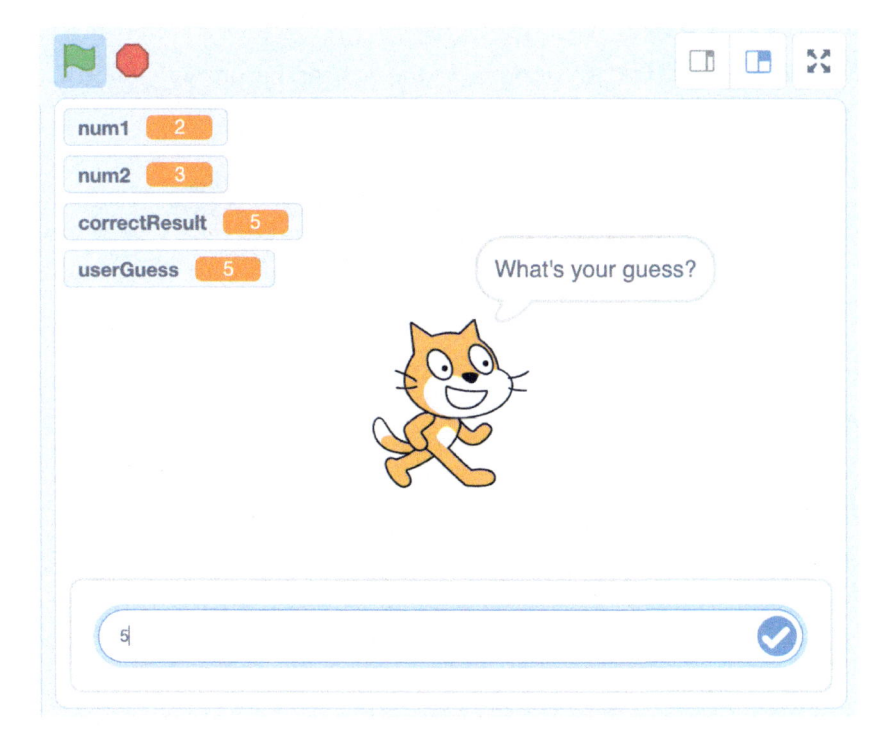

Perfect.

All that's left to do now is to check whether the user's guess was correct or not

and then show the appropriate message.

To execute different blocks depending on some condition, we need our "if then else" block.

Let's think about the condition - what do we need to check?

Well, obviously, whether the user's guess is correct. When is the guess considered correct?

If the "userGuess" variable is equal to the "correctResult" variable:

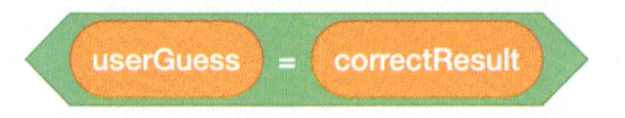

`[ userGuess = correctResult ]`

If that condition is *true*,

then we should say, "Yes that's correct!"

else, we say, "Sorry, the correct answer is:" and display the correct result:

Step 2 – How To Control The Flow

```
if  userGuess = correctResult  then
    say  Yes, that's correct!  for  2  seconds
else
    say  Sorry, the correct answer is:  for  1  seconds
    say  correctResult  for  1  seconds
```

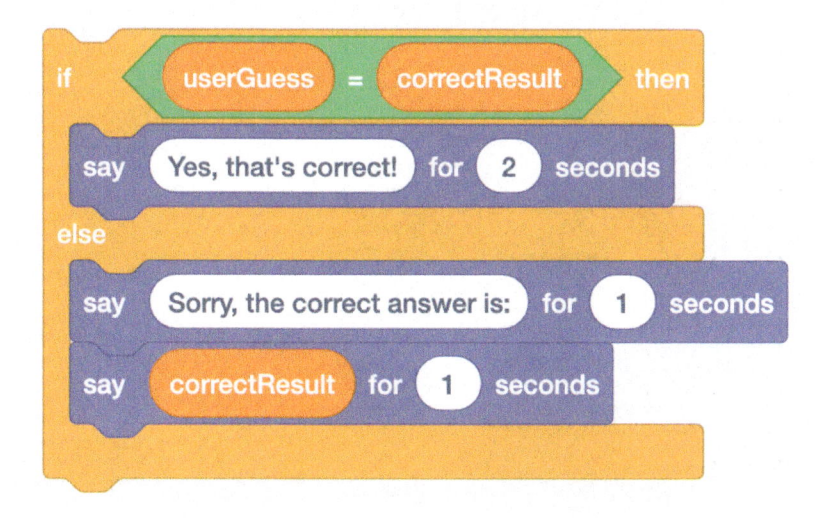

So, test this. Experiment with different user answers - the expected, correct result (5), and a couple of erroneous results. See whether you get the correct message back.

As a final step, let's replace the static values (2 and 3) in the first 2 blocks with the green "random" operator:

Operators

`pick random  1  to  10`

Every time you run the program now, you will get different numbers.

89

Here's the complete finished program:

```
when [flag] clicked
set num1 ▼ to (pick random 1 to 10)
set num2 ▼ to (pick random 1 to 10)
set correctResult ▼ to (num1 + num2)
ask (join (join (join num1 "+") num2) "= ?") and wait
set userGuess ▼ to (answer)
if <userGuess = correctResult> then
    say (Yes, that's correct!) for 2 seconds
else
    say (join (Sorry, the correct answer is: ) correctResult) for 2 seconds
```

(As you can see, I replaced the 3 "say" blocks at the top with the exercise given directly in the "ask" block. Additionally, I *join*ed the value of correctResult into a single "say" block at the bottom. Of course, both modifications are optional.)

Again, test this with different numbers for the guess.

Step 2 – How To Control The Flow

The only thing that is left to do is uncheck all the variable checkboxes:

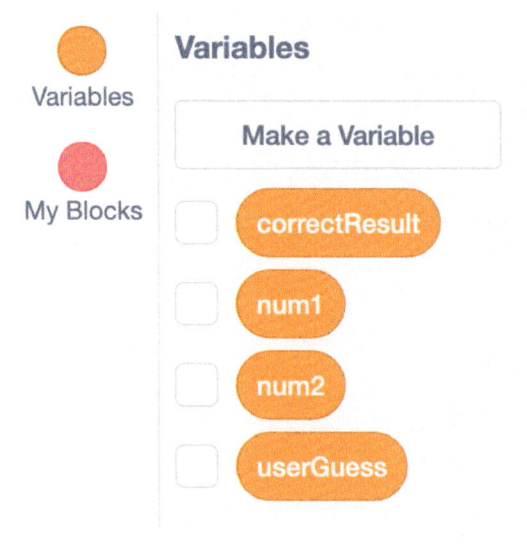

Variables

Make a Variable

correctResult

num1

num2

userGuess

Doing this will hide all the debug information of our variable values in the stage area (otherwise the exercise is not really hard to solve, since the user would see the "correctResult" value immediately):

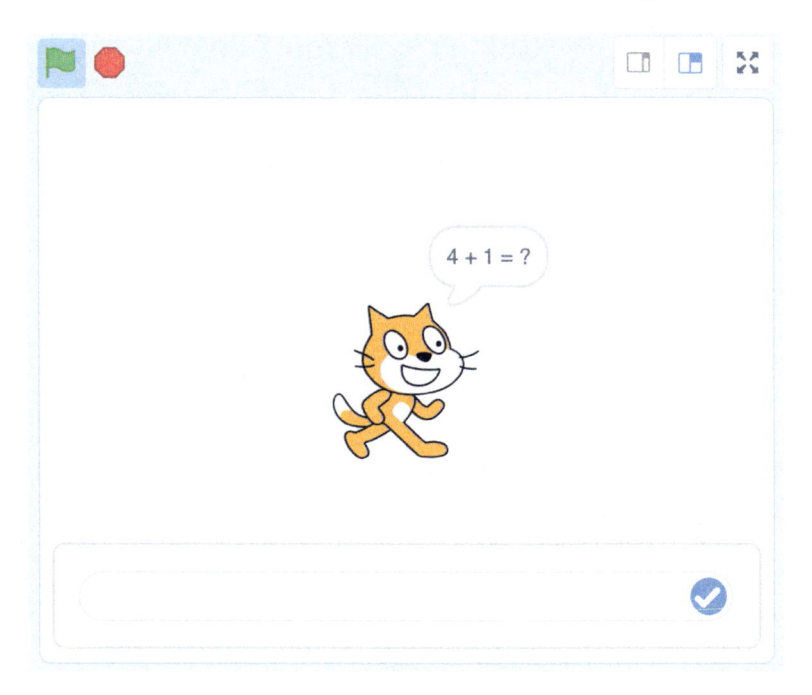

4 + 1 = ?

91

◆ ◆ ◆

So, that's it for this chapter.

Make sure to save this project by giving it a name and selecting "File" – "Save now."

Next, let's learn about loops.

How To Do Things More Than Once

Let's talk about another essential concept to control the flow in our program.

Our programs so far have been executed from top to bottom, and each block was executed only once.

Sometimes, it's useful to execute a particular part of our program multiple times.

We can achieve that by using a structure called a **loop**.

A loop lets us execute one or more blocks numerous times in our program.

Let's try that out:

In your list of Scratch blocks, scroll to the orange "Control" section (or click on the "Control" button to the left).

You've got a few different types of loops available - but right now, we want to use this one:

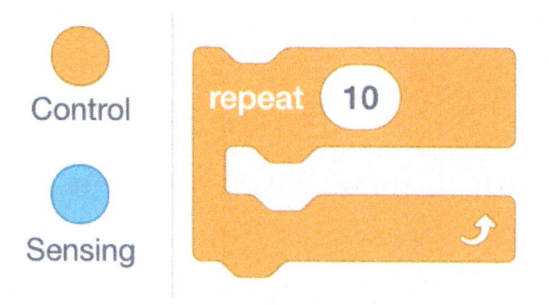

The "repeat" loop.

Like the "if then" block, the loop block looks like a bracket - that means you can drag blocks into the loop. Everything that's contained within that loop bracket will be executed multiple times.

How often?

Well, we specify that in the loop "header" at the top.

10 loop iterations is the default, but like with any round shape, you can change it.

So, let's try this out. Create the following program:

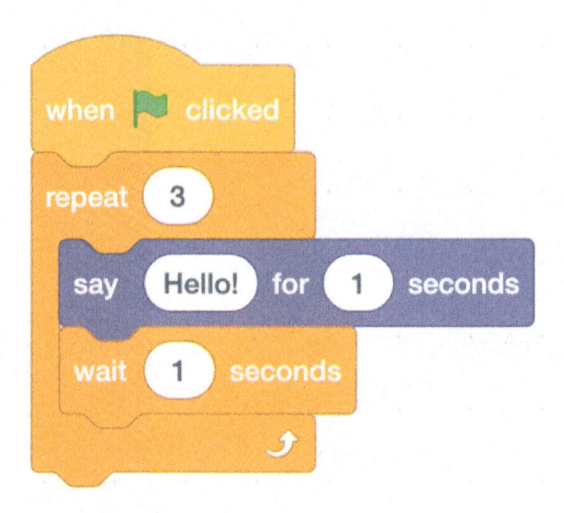

```
when [flag] clicked
repeat (3)
    say (Hello!) for (1) seconds
    wait (1) seconds
```

Note: We have not used the "wait" block before, but it's easy to figure out what it does, right? ... Yes, it just waits for the given number of seconds. (We are doing this to be able to see each "Hello" message separately.)

Run the program and count how many "Hello!" messages you see.

Next, change the number 3 to 5 and rerun the program.

Easy, right?

Everything inside the loop is called the "loop body."

All the blocks in the loop body will be executed multiple times - but note that inside the loop body, the execution goes step by step, from top to bottom, as always).

You might be thinking to yourself, "No big deal, Tom... We could have just used 3 or 5 "say (Hello!)" blocks."

Well, let's make things more interesting, shall we?

We create a "loop counter."

This is an essential concept that we need throughout all kinds of software development:

Executing the loop body multiple times and counting how often we are "iterating" (repeating the loop body).

So let's create a variable called "counter." (You know the drill by now: Click on "Variables," click on "Make a variable," and name it "counter.")

First, before doing anything else, let's initialize the counter variable with a starter value of 0:

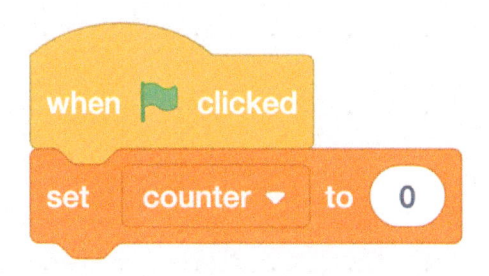

We want to use this counter variable to count up from 1 to 3.

You already know that we can output the current value of the variable simply by using it in a "say" block, like this:

`say [counter] for (1) seconds`

Quickly run this to see the output of "0" (the value of the counter variable).

To change the value, we can use a "change" block:

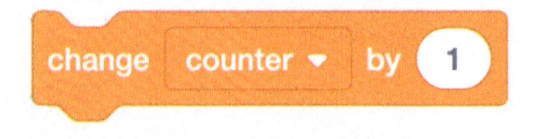

`change [counter v] by (1)`

This adds 1 to the current value of the counter - in our case, the current value is 0 (because we have just initialized it to 0 above). After this "change" block, the value of "counter" will be 1.

Try this out:

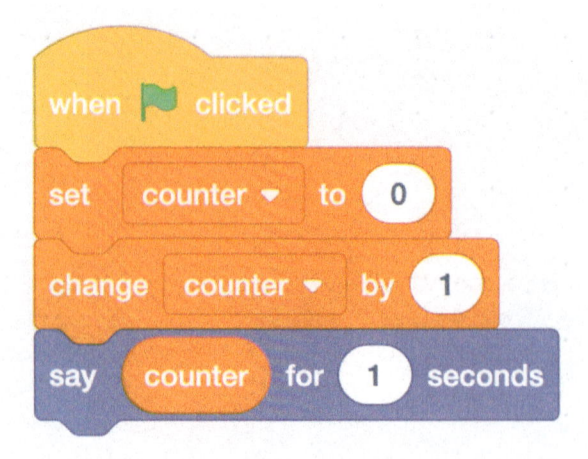

```
when [flag] clicked
set [counter v] to (0)
change [counter v] by (1)
say [counter] for (1) seconds
```

Run it and see "1" as output.

Now, if we would repeatedly execute the "change" and the "say" blocks repeatedly, we would be counting up, right?

But we don't want to duplicate those blocks.

Instead, let's put them into a "repeat" loop like this:

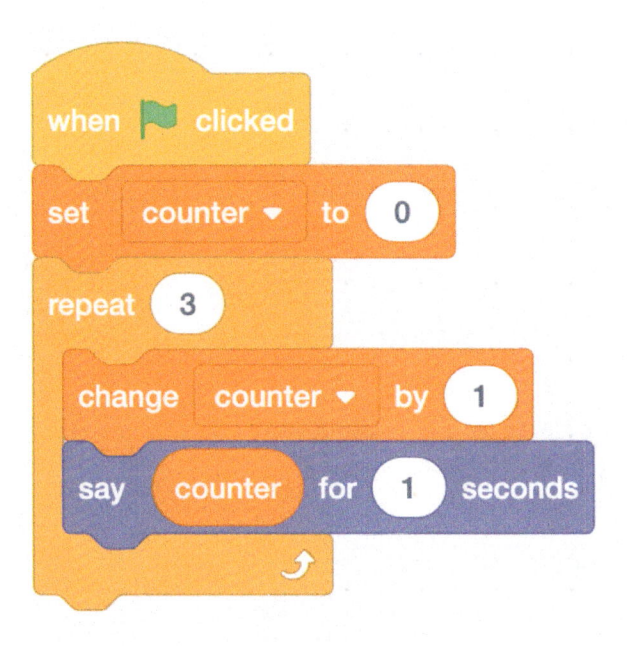

When you run this program, you will see your cat counting up from 1 to 3. After the loop has been executed 3 times, the program ends.

And you can easily change the number of repetitions by changing the number in the "repeat" block.

Try it - change it to 5 and rerun the program.

Let's take it one step further.

The cool thing with Scratch is that the shape always tells you what you can use where.

Like, any round shape can be used in any block that accepts a round shape inside.

Instead of always executing exactly 5 times, let's **ask** the user how far we should count up.

Can you do solve that puzzle by yourself?

Hint: You will need an "ask" block and the blue (**answer**) shape…

Here's the solution:

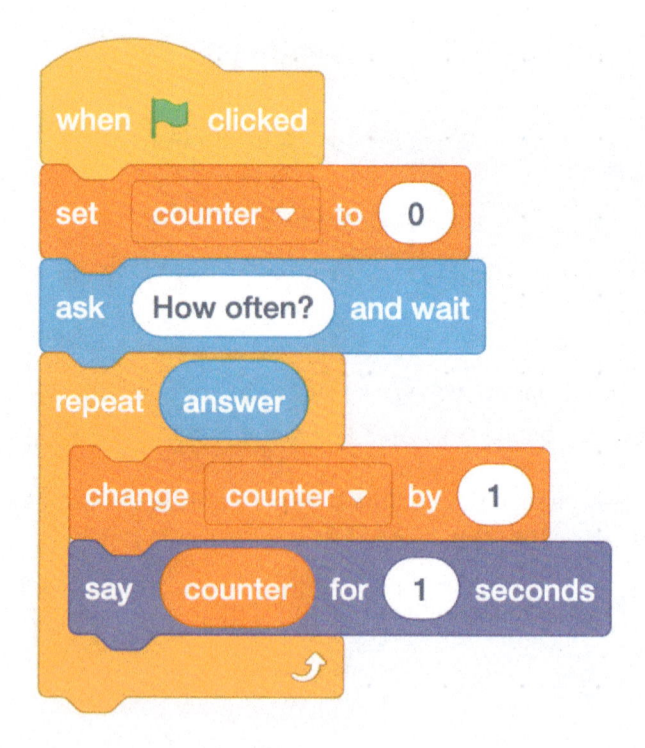

```
when [flag] clicked
set [counter ▼] to (0)
ask (How often?) and wait
repeat (answer)
    change [counter ▼] by (1)
    say (counter) for (1) seconds
end
```

Optionally, you could create a variable to store the user's answer, but here I'm just using the (answer) shape directly.

Run this a few times, and try out "weird" answers like 0, -5 or typing "five."

What did you find out?

Yes, only positive integer numbers work; otherwise the whole "repeat" loop is skipped.

As an exercise, what do you need to change if you want to count down from the user's number back to 1?

◆ ◆ ◆

In this lesson, we have learned a basic type of loop, the "repeat (times)" loop.

There are a few others in Scratch, like the "repeat until <condition>" loop - we will cover it in the next chapter.

Oh, and make sure to save this project by giving it a name and selecting "File" – "Save now."

EXTENDING OUR MATH QUIZ WITH LOOPS

Now that you learned about loops and "if then else" blocks, let's combine them.

Let's revisit our math quiz example that we've worked on before.

Here is where we left off:

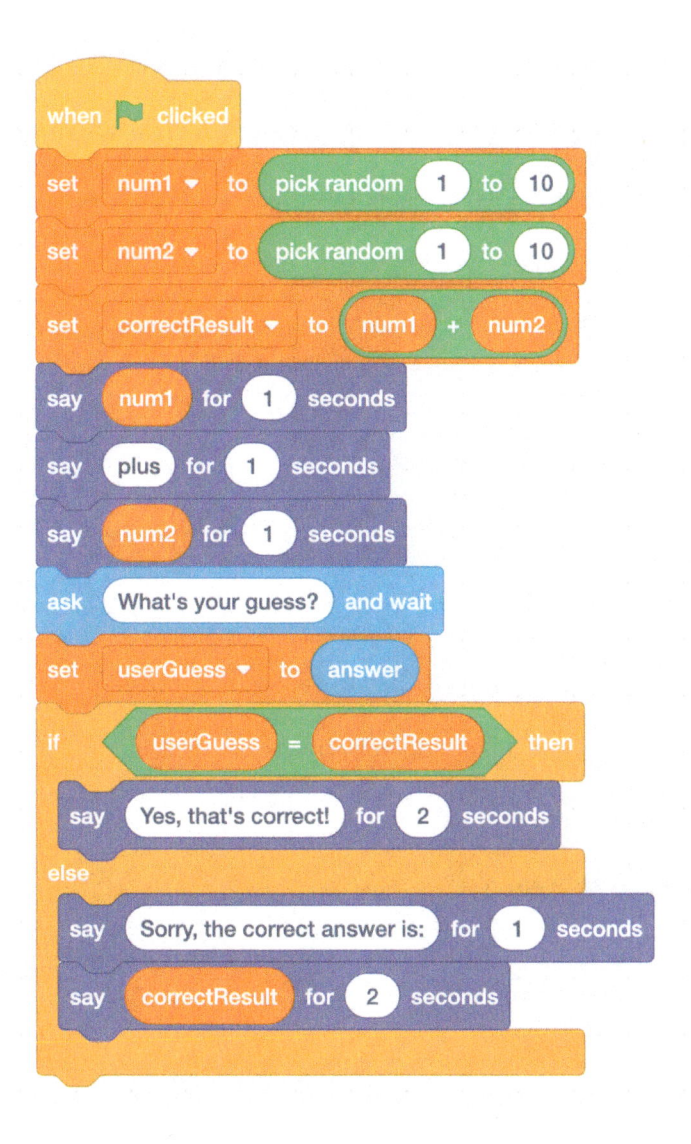

```
when [flag] clicked
set num1 to pick random 1 to 10
set num2 to pick random 1 to 10
set correctResult to num1 + num2
say num1 for 1 seconds
say plus for 1 seconds
say num2 for 1 seconds
ask What's your guess? and wait
set userGuess to answer
if <userGuess = correctResult> then
    say Yes, that's correct! for 2 seconds
else
    say Sorry, the correct answer is: for 1 seconds
    say correctResult for 2 seconds
```

Run the program to familiarize yourself with how it works. (You can check the checkboxes for the variables to see their values in the stage area.)

Now, let's extend this program.

Right now, we are asking the user for their guess only once.

Let's **repeat** this and ask the user again and again

until they have given the correct answer.

See what I did there?

Yes, we are going to use another type of loop:

The "repeat - until" loop:

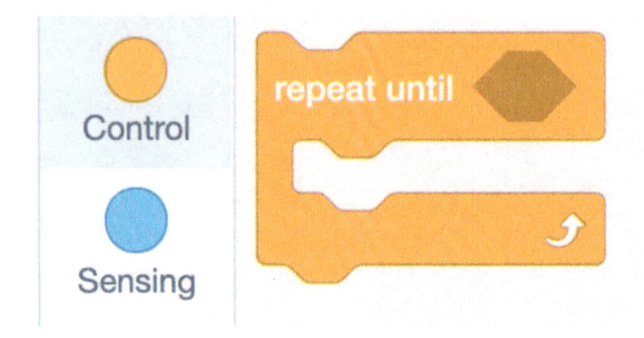

You will find the "repeat until" loop in the orange "Controls" section.

Drag it into the editor area, but do not attach it to anything just yet.

The question is:

Which blocks do we want to execute repeatedly?

The variables need to be initialized only once, and the "say" blocks with the exercise also should be executed just once - so these blocks will need to be outside the loop.

But asking the user for their guess and showing them the related message ("Yes that's correct" or "Sorry, try again") - <u>that's</u> the functionality we want to repeat until they have given the correct answer.

On a side note, we probably do not want to show the correct result in the "else" bracket, since that would defeat the purpose of letting them take another guess, right?

So, we move these blocks inside the "repeat until" loop, and modify the "else" branch, like this:

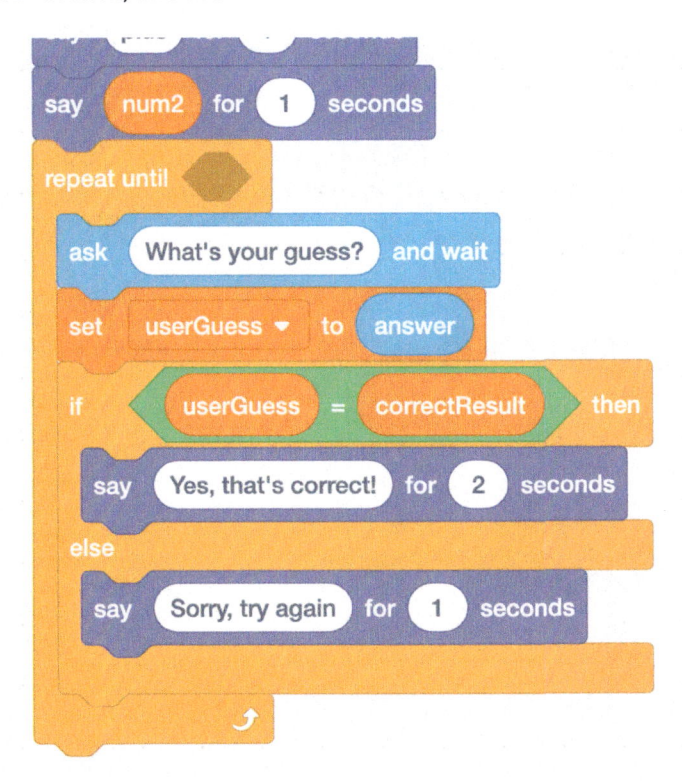

Notice: We've got two control structures nested inside each other:

The "repeat until" loop outside

and the "if / then / else" block inside the loop.

The remaining question is: What is the loop condition in the "repeat until <condition>" block going to be?

It is still empty:

![repeat until block with empty condition, above an ask "What's your guess?" block]

We want to repeat everything in the loop body until the user has entered the correct answer.

Note the difference to the "repeat (times)" loop we used in the previous chapter. In that case, we knew in advance how often the loop would be executed - because the number of repetitions is specified as a number.

With the "repeat until <condition>" loop, we do not know in advance how many loop repetitions it will take - it could be just one, it could be one thousand...

So... we repeat until the user's guess is correct. How can we check whether the user's guess is correct?

Well, we've got the "userGuess" and the "correctResult" variables.

We need a green "equals" comparison operator (with the pointy edges) to compare the user's guess - stored in the "userGuess" variable - with the actual correct result - stored in the "correctResult" variable.

Here's what it looks like:

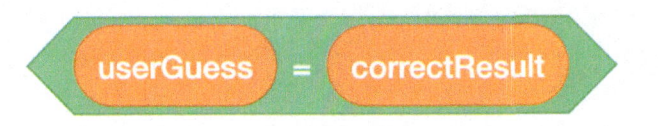

Yes, that's the same condition as in the "if"-statement!

Hint: If you are using a computer, you can right-click into the green shape of the if-condition, and then select "Duplicate":

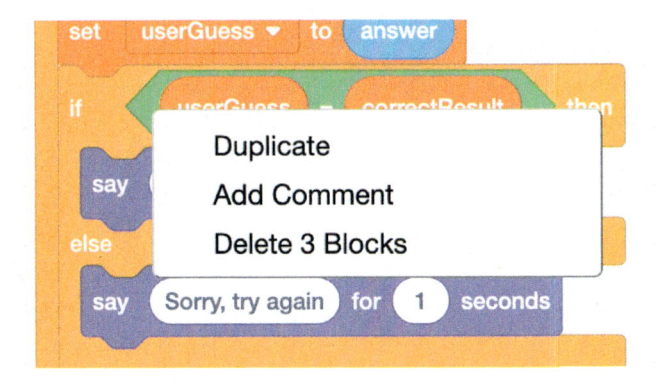

Drag the condition into the "repeat until" block.

Here's our advanced math quiz program so far:

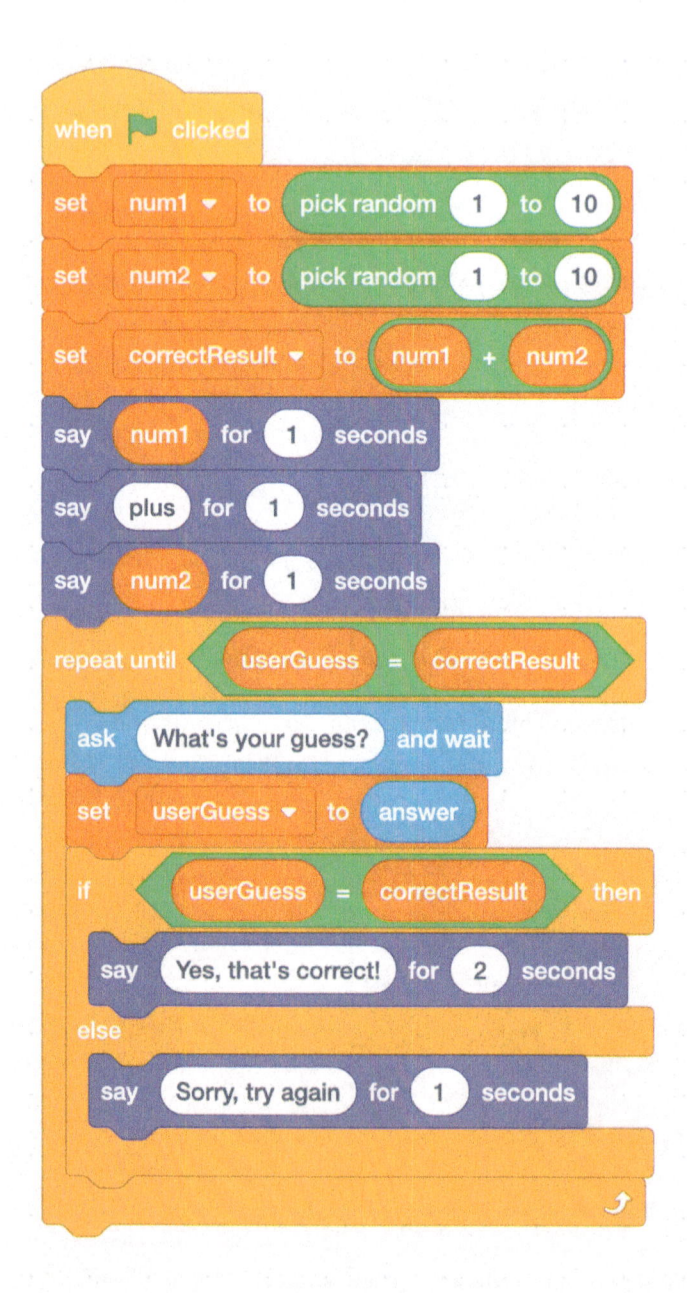

```
when [flag] clicked
set num1 to pick random 1 to 10
set num2 to pick random 1 to 10
set correctResult to num1 + num2
say num1 for 1 seconds
say plus for 1 seconds
say num2 for 1 seconds
repeat until userGuess = correctResult
    ask What's your guess? and wait
    set userGuess to answer
    if userGuess = correctResult then
        say Yes, that's correct! for 2 seconds
    else
        say Sorry, try again for 1 seconds
```

Run it and test it with different guesses.

Verify that the loop body is repeated as many times as necessary until you enter the correct result.

As an advanced exercise for you overachiever, let's do one more thing:

After the user has entered the correct result, let's show him how many guesses it took him (or her).

I'm going to leave that up to you, but here are a few hints:

- Make a "guessCounter" variable
- Set it to 0
- Change it by 1
- Say "Number of guesses" and the current value of the "guessCounter" variable

Think about where exactly you need to place each of these blocks - before the loop? Inside the loop? After the loop?

So, that's our math quiz advanced, using loops and using if-then-else statements.

◆ ◆ ◆

You've mastered step number two - controlling the flow of your program.

Congratulations!

Only one step remaining. See you in the next chapter!

STEP 3 – HOW TO CREATE BUILDING BLOCKS

Don't Repeat Yourself

This chapter covers the third and final step to master the basics of any programming language.

To recap just quickly:

Step one was learning how to manage data.

We have seen how we can get data into our program by using the "ask" block.

We have learned how to display data and get it out of our program, using the "say" or the "think" blocks.

We saw how we can process data using the green operator blocks - joining two texts together, doing basic math with the math operators.

The second step was learning how to control the flow in our program. We can specify a condition - for example, whether the value of a variable is equal to a specific value. If the condition is *true*, then we do one thing in our program, else we do another thing.

We have also seen how we can execute a part of our program multiple times using loops. In particular, we have used the "repeat (times)" and the "repeat until <condition>" loop.

We already used many different types of blocks that Scratch provides to us.

What's remaining is the third and probably most important step:

We learn how to define and use our own building blocks.

Creating our own blocks lets us reuse functionality.

We **define** our own custom block just **once**

but then can **use** and execute **many copies** of that block in different parts of our program.

Step 3 – How To Create Building Blocks

To understand what I mean by that, let's revisit one of the projects that we've worked on before, where we count up from a number one to a certain number:

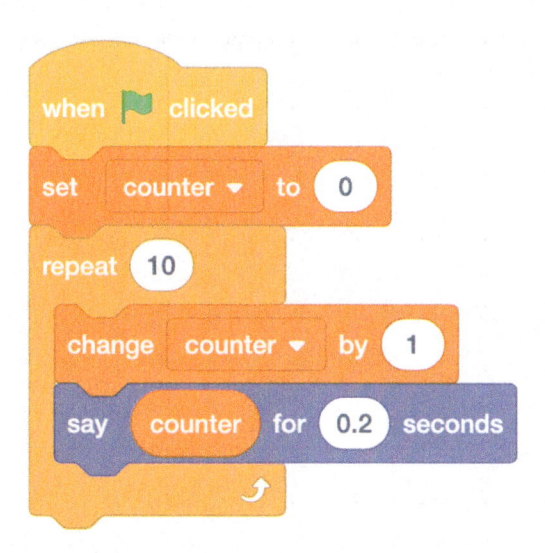

```
when [flag] clicked
set [counter ▼] to (0)
repeat (10)
    change [counter ▼] by (1)
    say (counter) for (0.2) seconds
end
```

Open this Scratch project and immediately click "File" - "Save as a copy".

(Or recreate it quickly - you will need a variable "counter.")

Of course, there's nothing new in here yet - we are just initializing the "counter" value to 0, so we ensure that we are starting from 0.

We repeat the loop body 10 times:

- Incrementing the value of "counter" by 1
- Output the current "counter" value with "say." (I have set the duration to 0.2 seconds so we don't have to wait too long for the program to complete.)

Run the program to make sure everything works as expected.

Now, let's make things interesting:

Let's pretend that we are writing a very long program, much bigger than this. And inside this long program, there are multiple places where we want to "count up."

Okay, we do not have such a long program yet - but let's just say we want to do this "count up" twice.

How would we achieve this?

Well - we could easily duplicate the existing blocks by right-clicking and selecting "Duplicate,":

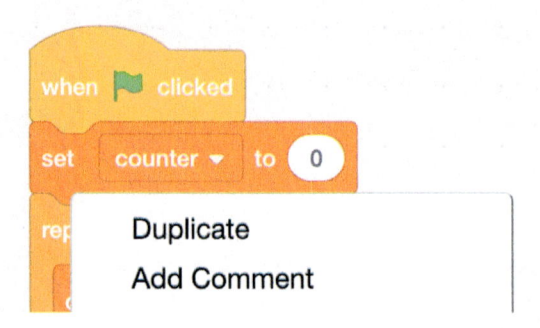

Step 3 – How To Create Building Blocks

So, do that now and connect your duplicate blocks like this:

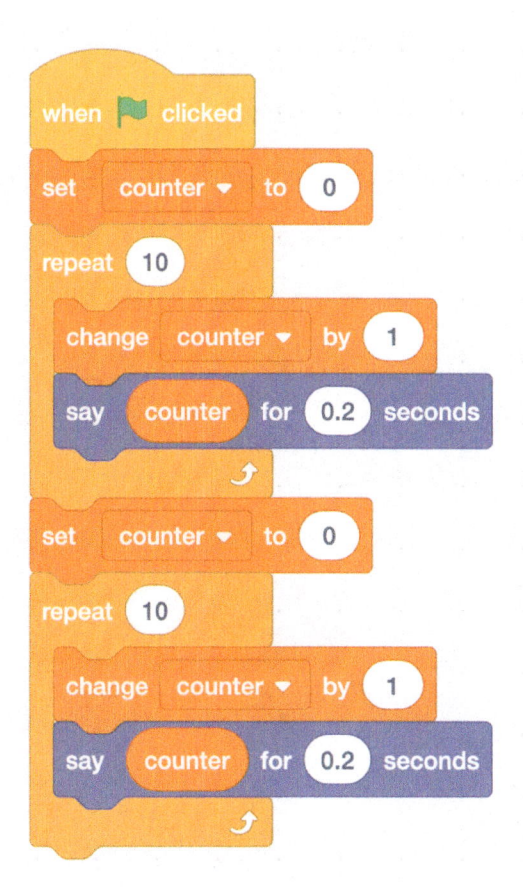

```
when [flag] clicked
set counter to 0
repeat 10
    change counter by 1
    say counter for 0.2 seconds
set counter to 0
repeat 10
    change counter by 1
    say counter for 0.2 seconds
```

Now, if I click "Go," we're going to count up from one to 10, twice.

Of course - no big deal, right? Well...

113

Think about this:

What if you want to change something in this "count-up" behavior? Let's pretend that you found a bug, and instead of counting to 10, you actually wanted to count to 5.

You would need to correct that "error" in every duplicated block one by one:

```
when [flag] clicked
set counter to 0
repeat 5
    change counter by 1
    say counter for 0.2 seconds
set counter to 0
repeat 5
    change counter by 1
    say counter for 0.2 seconds
```

That's nice, but now what if you want to show each message not 0.2 seconds, but 0.5 seconds instead?

Again, you'd have to repeat any modification in all the duplicated blocks.

So you would think, "Well, no big deal, right? I just do the modifications two times."

But what if you use that functionality not just twice but dozens or even hundreds of times in your (hypothetically long) program?

If you are asking yourself now, "Tom, why would I want to count up hundreds of times in your program?"...

In programming, you often want to do a specific operation multiple times - printing emails, moving dozens of files, sharing a list of photos with somebody...

And what we absolutely want to avoid is to duplicate or copy/paste code snippets multiple times throughout our programs.

Because if you need to change anything in this code snippet, you need to modify it numerous times (in all the places).

You must not forget a single location in your code where you need to change it. Otherwise, your program would behave erratically.

So it actually makes sense to say:

We don't want to copy/paste any code.

And because programmers love acronyms, they named this the **DRY principle - Don't Repeat Yourself**.

DEFINING YOUR NEW BLOCK

Instead of duplicating, let's **define** the "countUp" functionality only **once**.

Then everywhere we want to use that functionality, we just **use** that custom single block - but we do not copy/paste the actual block "implementation" (the internal workings that make up our custom functionality).

So that's the idea.

Let's see this in practice:

On the left, click on the pink "My Blocks" button, and then on "Make a Block":

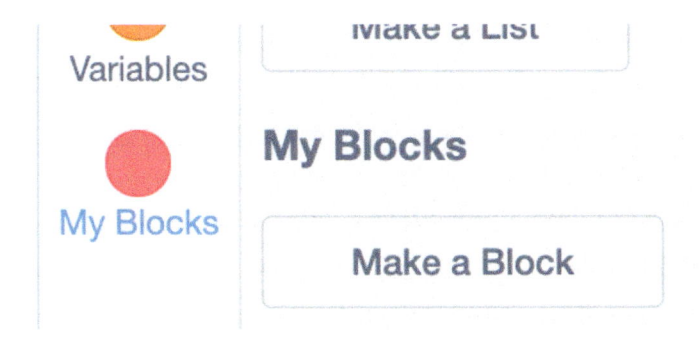

It's similar to the "Make a Variable" steps we've seen before.

First, we need to give our new block a name. Let's call it "countUp."

(Click in the white rectangle below the red trash can):

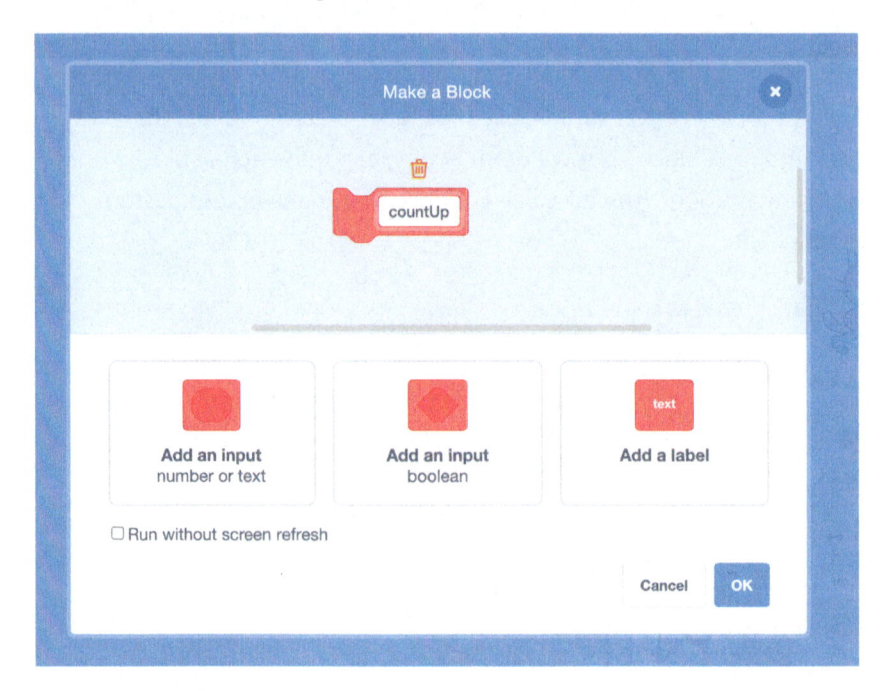

No need to change anything else, so just click "OK."

Two things happened:

First, under "My Blocks," a pink "countUp" block appeared:

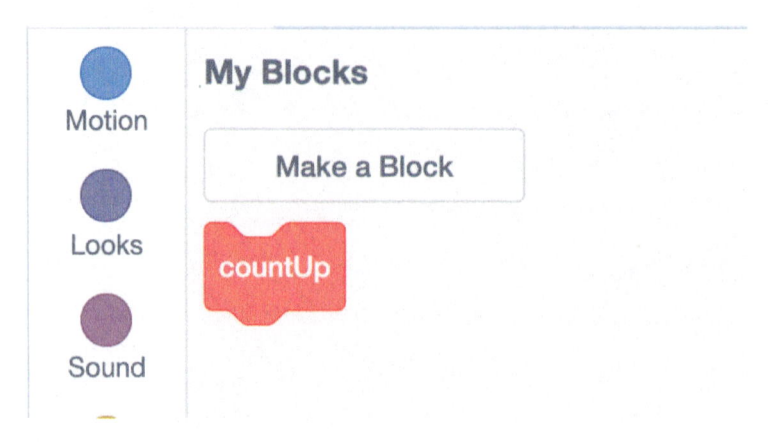

Second, in the editor area, we now got a red "define countUp" block:

That "define countUp" block looks a little bit like our "When the green flag is clicked" block - it has this shape at the bottom, so we can attach some blocks below it.

First, remove the duplicated blocks (just detach them and drag them over to the left, so they disappear).

Then, move the remaining blocks below the "define countUp" block like this:

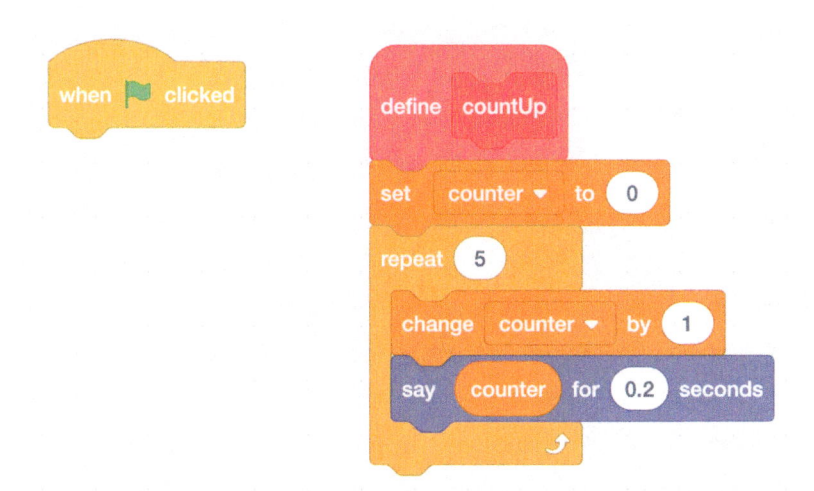

See what happens if you run this program...

Nothing happens.

Why? Because the main program below "When the green flag is clicked" is empty now – so there is nothing to execute.

The definition on the right is just, well – a definition.

Let's learn how to use our new block.

USING YOUR CUSTOM BLOCK

Similar to the variables, you can drag your new "countUp" block from the "My Blocks" section of the library into the editor area.

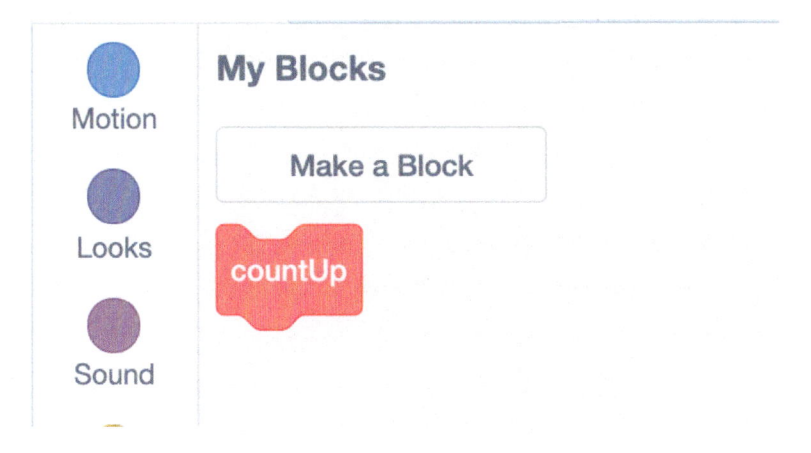

Drag it and attach it to the main program like this:

Note the difference:

Below "define countUp", we are **defining** our block.

On the left side, below "When the green flag is clicked", we are actually **using** our new block in the program - just like any other block.

Run the program and check what happens - it should be counting up from 1 to 5.

Let's modify the program to wait and call "countUp" a second time, like this:

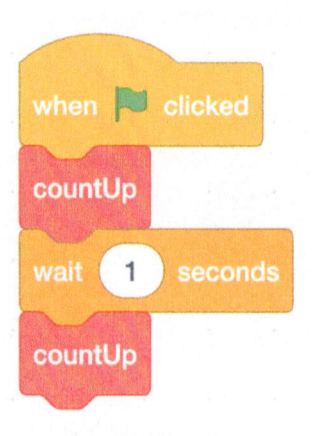

[Scratch blocks: when green flag clicked → countUp → wait 1 seconds → countUp]

Run the modified program now.

Notice the yellow outline? It jumps between the main program and the "define countUp" block to show which part is currently executing.

What if you find a bug - for example, the counter messages are too quick for your taste, and you want to show them for 1 second instead of 0.2 seconds?

Now you need to make this change just once in the block definition - and not multiple times as before with our manually duplicated blocks.

Or, say you want to count to 15 instead of 5. You can also change this just once in the definition. Every time the "countUp" block is executed, it will count to 15 instead of 5.

That also means you have to search for any problems or errors only once - inside your block definition. If you know that it works one time, it will work every time you use that block.

◆ ◆ ◆

Okay, so that's the idea of creating your own building blocks.

This is really fundamental to all modern programming languages - we don't call them "blocks" there, but "functions" or "methods," but the idea is the same:

You define your functionality once, and then you can use it many times from multiple places in your program.

Next, let's expand on this topic and learn how to make our own blocks even more flexible and valuable.

BLOCKS WITH PARAMETERS

Let's make things (even) more interesting.

Currently, we are counting from one to 15 because that's the way we've defined our "countUp" block (on the right):

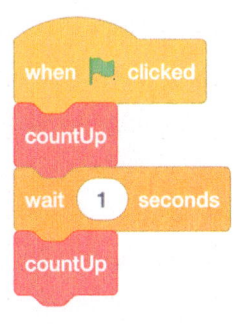

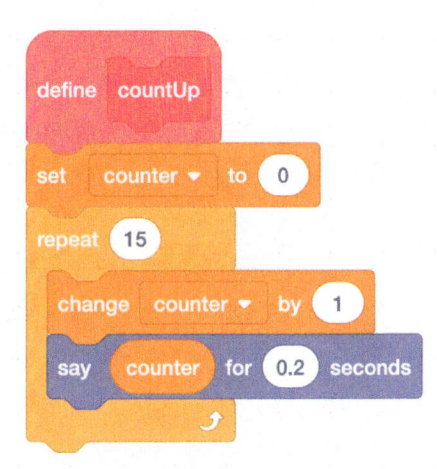

(Depending on your code, the number of loop repetitions might differ. But the important fact here is that it's ALWAYS the same number, with every call of "countUp.")

Now let's assume we do not always want to count to precisely the same value every time.

But we still do not wish to duplicate any code (DRY - "Don't Repeat Yourself", remember?)

How can we achieve this?

Well, we have come across a similar situation before. Do you remember this program?

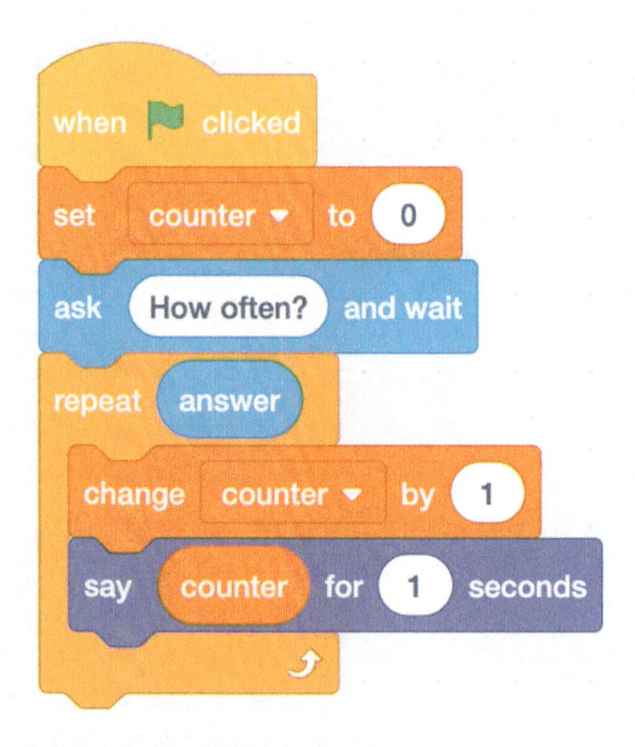

```
when [flag] clicked
set counter to 0
ask How often? and wait
repeat answer
    change counter by 1
    say counter for 1 seconds
```

We asked the user how often the program should repeat the loop. The (answer) shape specified the number to count up to.

We can do a similar thing with custom blocks.

Let's create another custom block.

Step 3 – How To Create Building Blocks

Click on "My Blocks" and then "Make a Block."

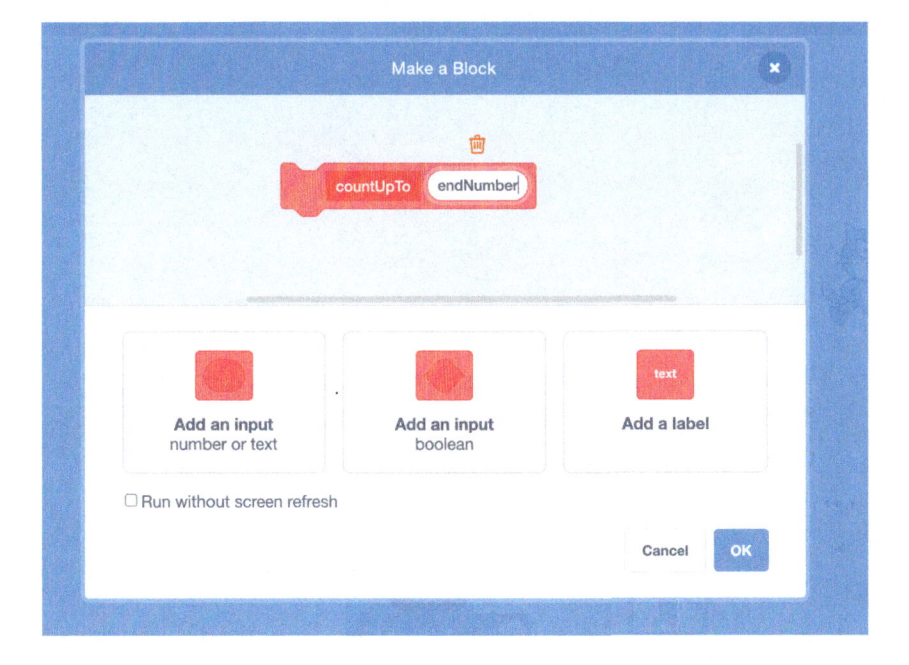

Name the new block "countUpTo".

This is important: Click the "Add an input" button in the lower-left, and name the round shape "endNumber."

Click "OK."

Here's what you see:

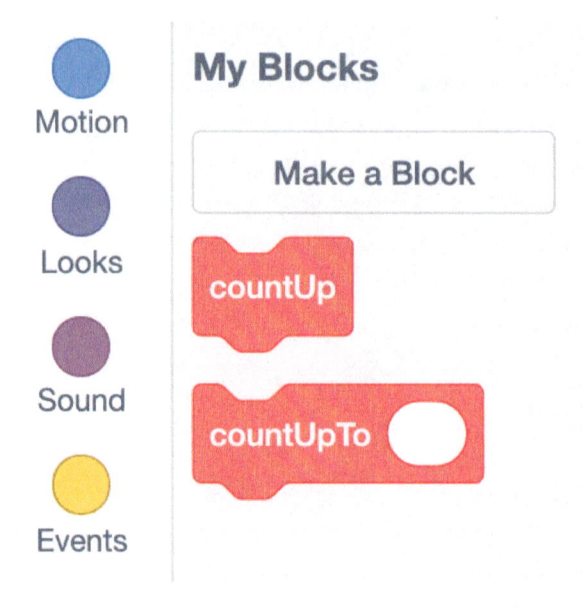

First, under "My Blocks," you see the new block "countUpTo" you have just created - **and it has a round shape next to it!**

Interesting.

Also, you see a "define" block in the editor area, and it has this "endNumber" parameter that we specified inside a round shape:

What is this "endNumber" shape?

Step 3 – How To Create Building Blocks

It is a special variable (called a "parameter") that you can use inside the definition of your "countUpTo" block.

Can you guess what you need to do with it?

Well, let's start by copying the blocks from our previous "countUp" block definition (simply right-click and select "Duplicate"), and drag the duplicated blocks below the definition of our new "countUpTo" block.

(Note: I know we said we don't want to duplicate code - but I want to show you the difference between the two custom block definitions, side by side, so it's okay to duplicate in this case.)

These are the blocks you need to duplicate:

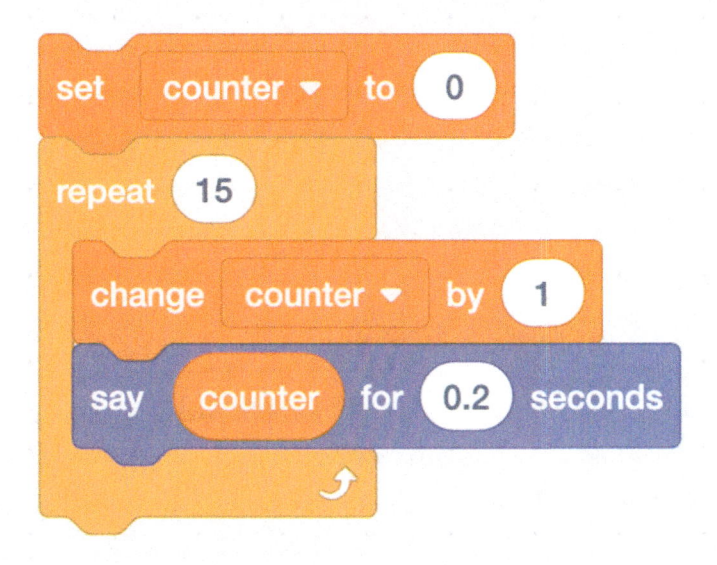

```
set counter to 0
repeat 15
    change counter by 1
    say counter for 0.2 seconds
```

Drag these duplicated blocks below the definition of your new "countUpTo" block.

129

Next, modify the repeat loop.

Drag-and-drop the "endNumber" shape and drop it next to "repeat" so it looks like this:

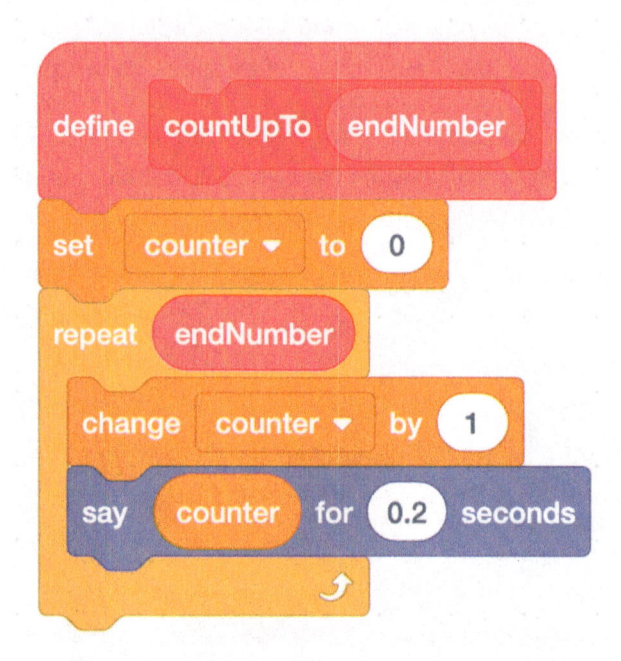

```
define countUpTo endNumber
    set counter to 0
    repeat endNumber
        change counter by 1
        say counter for 0.2 seconds
```

If you would click "run" right now, you wouldn't execute your new "countUpTo" block yet - because we are not calling it yet. We have simply just defined it.

So, drag two "countUpTo" blocks from the library on the left to create your new program.

Here's my example:

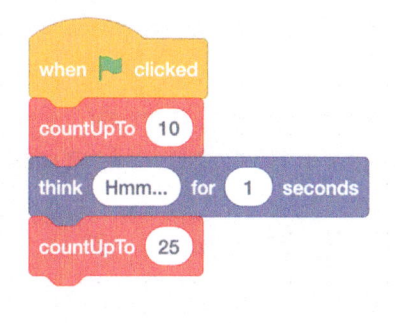

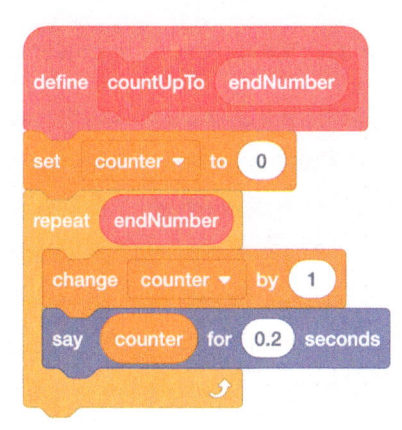

You will need to specify the "endNumber" value for each block, but here's the kicker: **The numbers can differ**.

So in my example, I'm giving it a value of 10 for (endNumber) - so it's counting from 1 to 10.

And the second time, I'm calling "countUpTo" with 25 - so the counter goes from 1 to 25.

Two different behaviors - although it's the exact same block definition.

Do you get the idea?

Each time we call our "countUpTo" block, we can customize what it actually does by handing it an "endNumber" parameter.

This concept is very, very important.

Without parameters, your custom block will do precisely the same every time you use it. This can still be useful to avoid code duplication.

But with parameters, you can actually have your block do different things depending on the input parameter you're giving it

while still defining the block only once.

This makes your code more universally usable.

You can be building your own library of your custom blocks, your own custom functionalities, and you have the option to customize each call of your block with parameters.

Got that? Cool!

Let's do an actual exercise where you will create and use your own custom blocks!

PLAYING A NUMBER GUESSING GAME

Now let's create a bigger project, using everything we have learned so far.

This time, I will show you the outcome first - the output of the program we want to create.

The user's perspective

The program is a simple game in which the computer selects a random number, and the user has to guess the correct number. The computer hints whether the guess is too high, too low, or correct.

This is the start of the program:

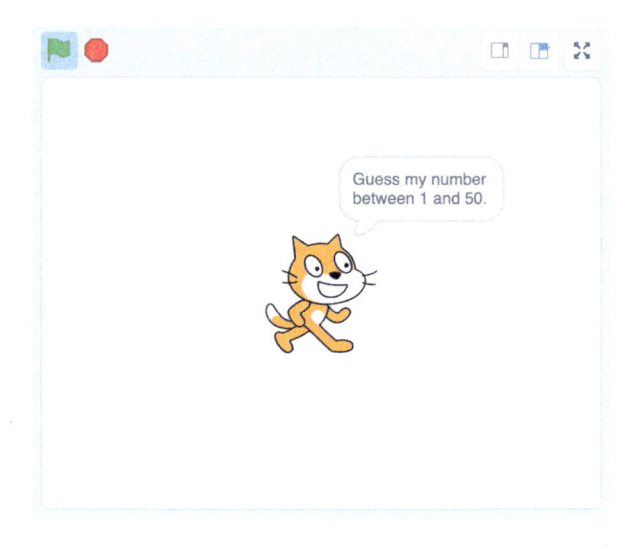

The user enters their first guess. Let's say it's 22:

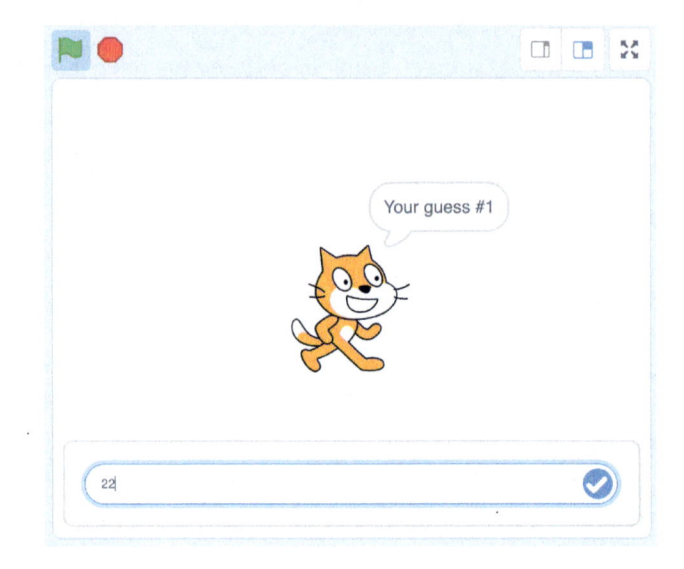

Next, the program tells the user whether the guess has been too low

or too high

or if they have indeed found the correct number.

In this particular case, the guess has been too low, so the program informs the user:

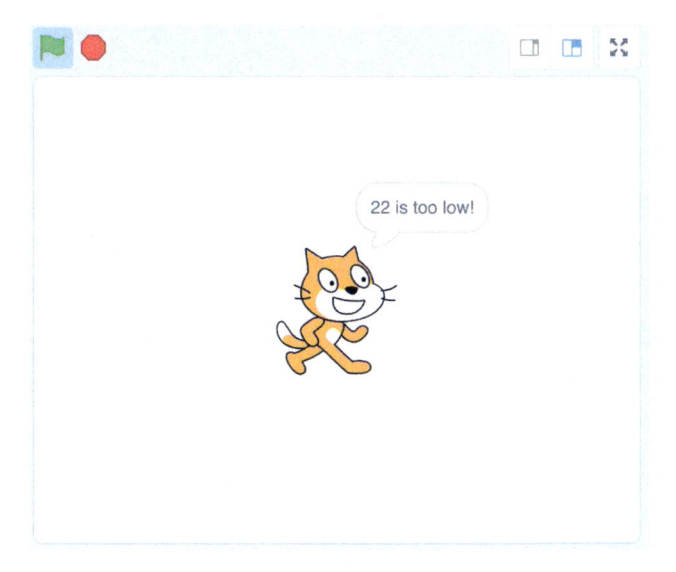

If the correct number has not been found yet, the user is asked for their next guess:

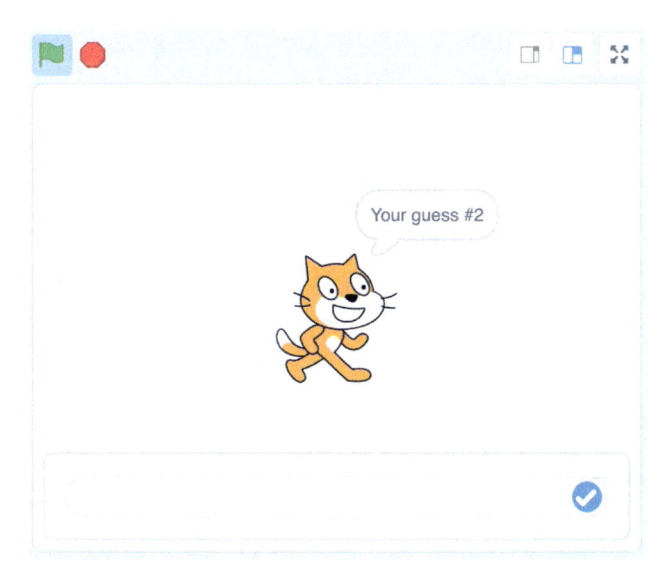

135

If the guess is too high, the user sees this message:

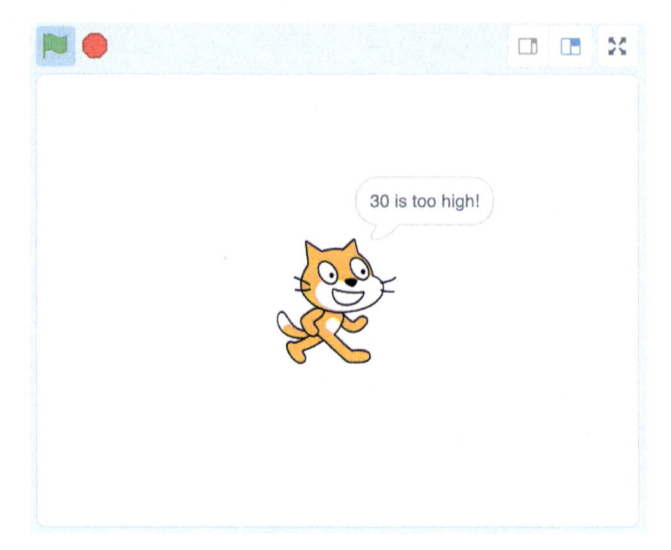

30 is too high!

This repeats until the user has found the correct number, in which case the number of guesses is displayed, and the program ends.

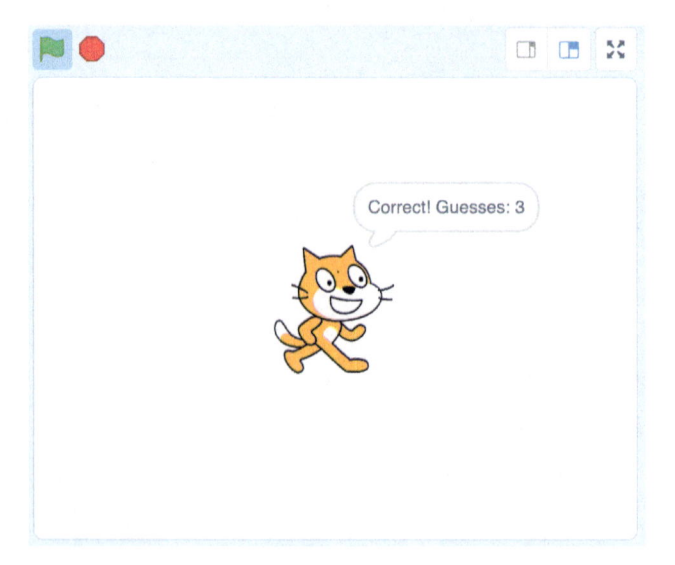

Correct! Guesses: 3

Okay, so that's the program from the user's point of view.

Creating the program

Let's think about what you need to do to create what we have seen.

I will give you some ideas and hints, but you should really try this by yourself first before looking at the solution in the next chapter.

Here's the single most important tip:

Don't try to implement everything at once. Instead, break down the functionality.

Need more help?

Ask yourself: What's the simplest thing you could do first?

Maybe - creating a variable for the number to guess and then set it to a random value. This is just a single line of code, and you know how to do this.

So, create the variable, **set** it to a random value, and then run this single line.

Make sure you have the checkbox next to your variable checked, and observe the debug info in the stage area that the variable's value has been set correctly, and that it changes every time you run the program.

Only if that works, take the next step.

Continue by **ask**ing the user for his guess.

Don't worry about the loop yet - just ask for the first guess.

Next, create a variable for the user's guess, and **set** it to the user's **answer**.

Again, run the program in its current state, and test that this variable is set correctly.

Only if that works, take the next step:

Check **if** the user's guess has been lower than the correct number - if so, **then** you **say** something like "Too low!".

Also, add a check **if** the guess has been higher, **then** you **say** a different message in that case.

And the last check is **if** the guess has been correct - **then** you **say** a third kind of message.

Now, run the program, enter a number and check whether you get the right message back.

Test it for all three cases.

And once you see the right message - "too high," "too low," or "correct" - then you're pretty much done with the first part.

The second part follows:

You need to keep repeating this "ask and say too high / to low / correct" part of your program.

So you're going to **repeat until** the user has actually guessed the correct number.

That's the second step.

And if that's working, and only if that's working, you worry about the counter.

You create a counter variable, you **set** it to 0,

change it by 1 inside the loop,

and then **say** the value at the end.

◆ ◆ ◆

You already know everything necessary to complete this exercise.

The most important thing is what I just described:

Learning how to decompose a problem and break it into smaller parts, into simpler sub-problems.

You then solve each sub-problem, one by one, and test the solution to ensure that everything still works as expected.

And only then do you tackle the next sub-problem and solve it.

Don't just code everything at once and hope that it's working.

You keep building up stuff, testing every new step, and only continue when the current step is working as expected.

You got this. You can do it.

Just take it step by step - start with a single block, test it and see what happens. Add another block. Look at the variable values.

And once you've got your solution, or maybe you need some help, continue with the next chapter, where I'm showing you a possible solution.

Programming Your Number Guessing Game

So, did you get it?

Before I show you my solution, it's essential to realize that there is no *perfect* solution or "the" solution.

If your program does what it's supposed to be doing, then it doesn't really matter that much how your program looks like - at least for our intents and purposes right now.

Here's my way of solving this exercise:

First of all, I have split this into two parts - the main program and a custom "showMessage" block.

You don't have to do it that way, but I wanted to use everything that we've learned so far.

Main program

Let's look at the main program first:

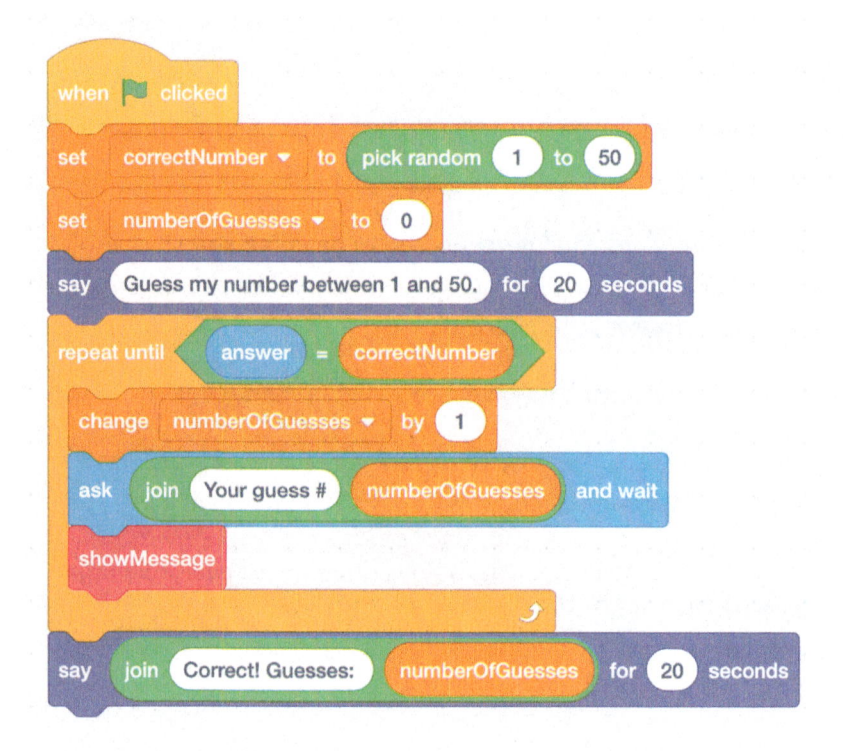

```
when 🏁 clicked
set correctNumber ▼ to pick random 1 to 50
set numberOfGuesses ▼ to 0
say Guess my number between 1 and 50. for 20 seconds
repeat until answer = correctNumber
    change numberOfGuesses ▼ by 1
    ask join Your guess # numberOfGuesses and wait
    showMessage
say join Correct! Guesses: numberOfGuesses for 20 seconds
```

I have created two variables - "correctNumber" and "numberOfGuesses":

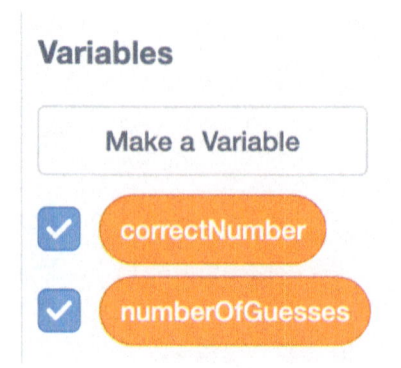

Variables

Make a Variable

☑ correctNumber

☑ numberOfGuesses

"correctNumber" is the number we want the user to find. We set it to a random number between 1 and 50, using the green "pick random" operator.

"numberOfGuesses" is used to count the number of guesses that the user has taken so far, and we set it to the initial value of 0:

```
when [flag] clicked
set correctNumber to pick random 1 to 50
set numberOfGuesses to 0
```

We are showing the game instructions to the user with a "say" block.

The next part is the loop - let's just look at the loop body for now:

```
change numberOfGuesses by 1
ask join (Your guess #) (numberOfGuesses) and wait
showMessage
```

All we are doing in the loop is these 3 things:

- First, we add 1 to the "numberOfGuesses" variable.
- Next, we ask the user for his guess.
- Lastly, we are calling the custom "showMessage" block. (Let's ignore that for now, I will cover that soon)

And we are **repeat**ing these 3 blocks over and over again,

until the answer that the user has given is equal to the value of "correctNumber":

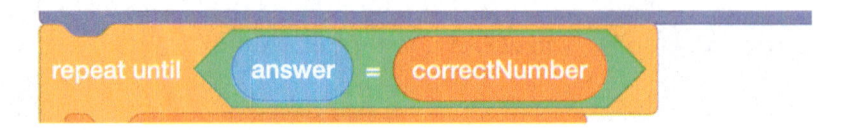

```
repeat until   answer = correctNumber
```

Easy as that.

As soon as this condition is true, the whole loop is skipped, and we continue with the last "say" block:

```
say  join  Correct! Guesses:  numberOfGuesses  for  2  seconds
```

Then the program ends.

The custom "showMessage" block

So, what's going on in the "showMessage" block?

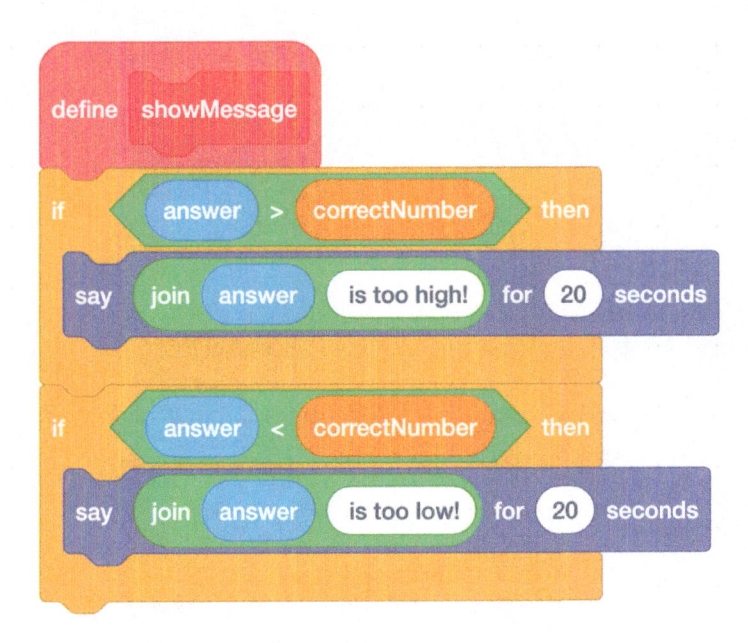

```
define showMessage
    if  answer > correctNumber  then
        say join answer is too high!  for 20 seconds

    if  answer < correctNumber  then
        say join answer is too low!  for 20 seconds
```

The block definition does not use a parameter; it uses the (answer) shape of the "ask" block from the main program.

(That works, although one could argue that it's cleaner to use a parameter for that block, so we can hand over the user's answer explicitly... But it's good enough for now.)

Then, we have two if statements - one for the "too low" case, the other one for the "too high" case.

Are you wondering why I'm using two separate "if" statements here - and not just one "if then else" block?

Let's think this through. This is how a single "if then else" block would look like:

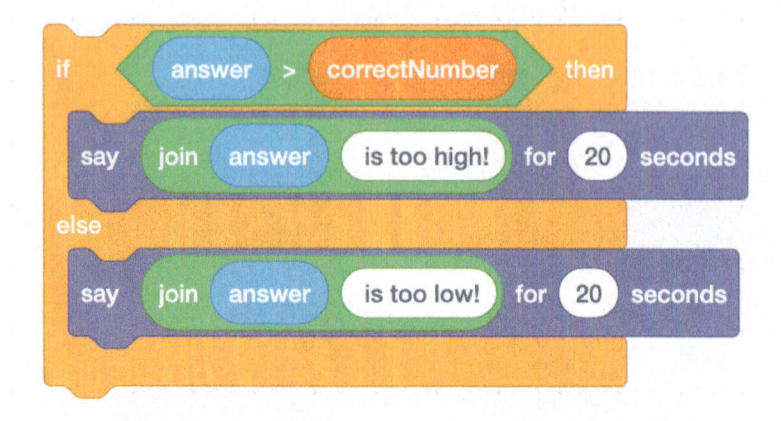

```
if  < answer > correctNumber >  then
    say  join  answer  is too high!  for  20  seconds
else
    say  join  answer  is too low!  for  20  seconds
```

What happens in the case that the user guesses correctly?

Well, if the user's answer is indeed correct, the "if" condition has to be false:

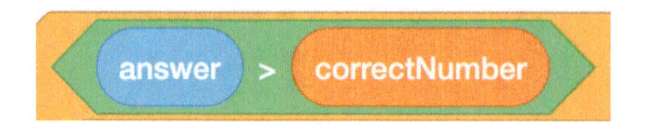

```
< answer > correctNumber >
```

Why? Because the value of "answer" is not greater than "correctNumber" - it is, in fact, equal to correctNumber.

And since the if-condition is false, we execute the "else" branch...

```
else
    say  join  answer  is too low!  for  20  seconds
```

... where we say "(answer) is too low" - which is obviously wrong since the answer is actually correct, not too low.

That's why we need two separate "if" statements here.

Take your time with this exercise and the solution.

Play around with it, experiment with it, modify blocks, rearrange them, intentionally break the logic of the program, understand why it's broken, and then fix it again.

As with everything else, practice makes perfect.

Here's my complete solution:

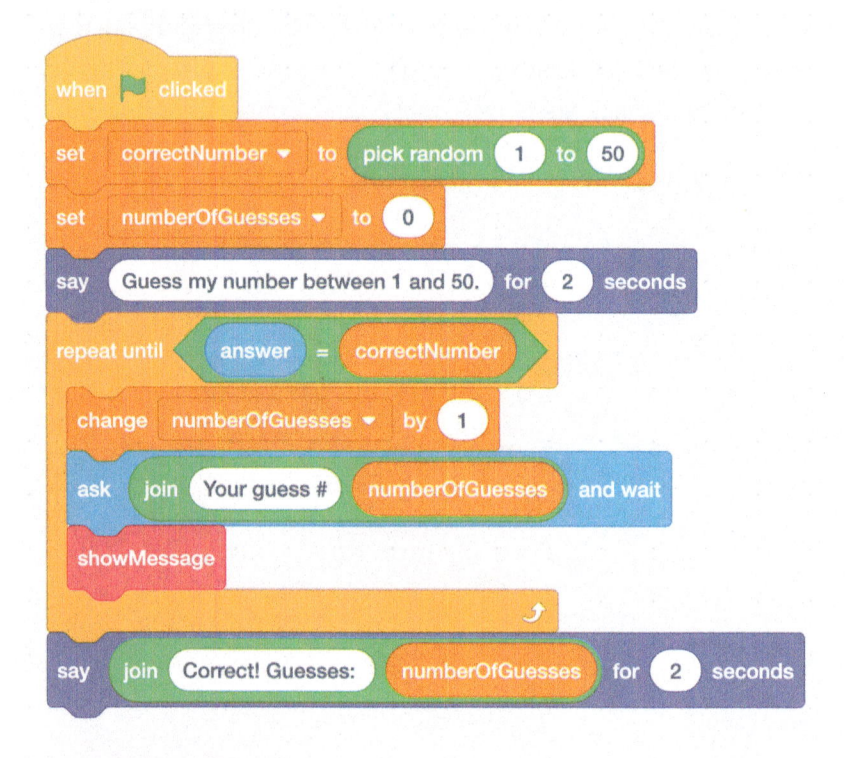

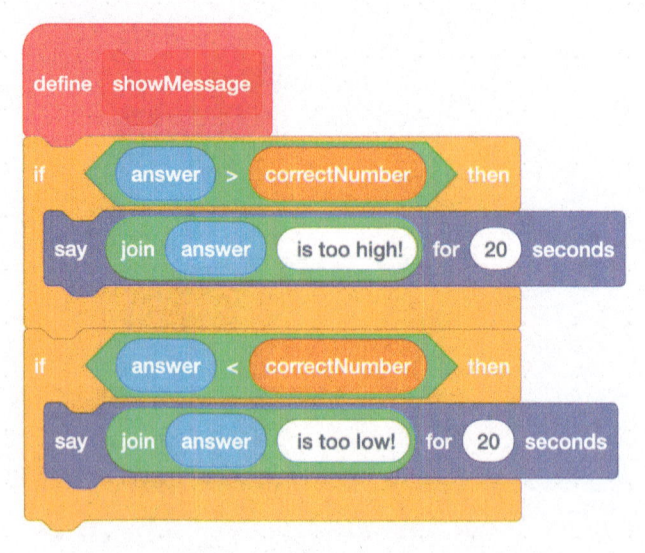

```
when [flag] clicked
set [correctNumber ▼] to (pick random (1) to (50))
set [numberOfGuesses ▼] to (0)
say (Guess my number between 1 and 50.) for (2) seconds
repeat until <(answer) = (correctNumber)>
    change [numberOfGuesses ▼] by (1)
    ask (join (Your guess #) (numberOfGuesses)) and wait
    showMessage
end
say (join (Correct! Guesses:) (numberOfGuesses)) for (2) seconds
```

```
define showMessage
if <(answer) > (correctNumber)> then
    say (join (answer) (is too high!)) for (20) seconds
end
if <(answer) < (correctNumber)> then
    say (join (answer) (is too low!)) for (20) seconds
end
```

EVEN MORE BLOCKS

EXTENSIONS

By now, you've probably realized that Scratch is really special. It lets you concentrate on the logic itself without worrying about difficult-to-remember syntax.

And it allows you to do things that would be much more complicated in other languages.

Many more blocks are available to us, but they are hidden by default when you create a new project.

Let's change that.

Create a new project, and look at the bottom of the list of block categories, where you see this blue "Add Extension" icon with the little +:

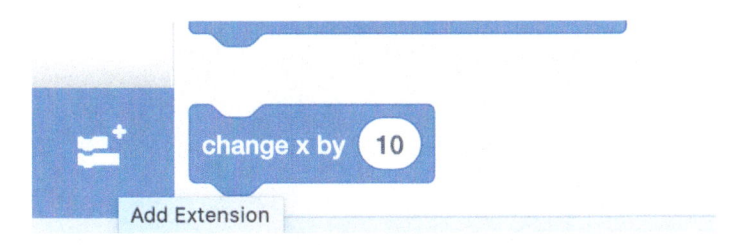

Click on "Add Extension", and you see a screen with many extensions that you can use to extend the functionality of Scratch. Each extension makes specific additional Scratch blocks available to you.

Let me show you an example:

BUILD YOUR OWN SIRI / ALEXA

After you click the blue "Add Extension" button on the left of your editor, find the "Text to Speech" extension:

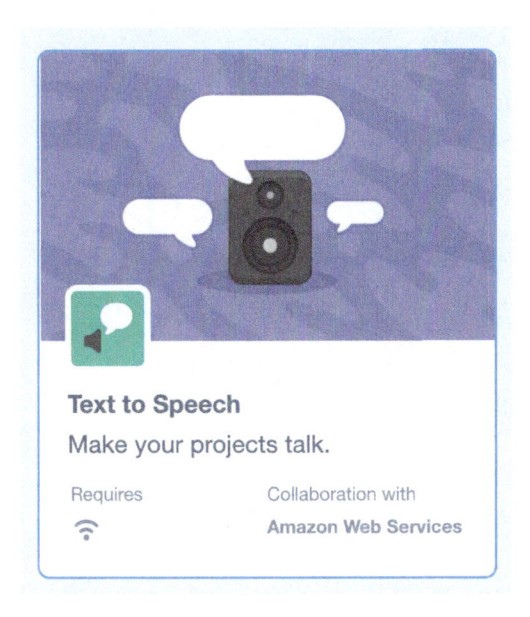

Text to Speech
Make your projects talk.

Requires 📶
Collaboration with **Amazon Web Services**

This extension provides us a couple of new blocks that allow your program to "talk" to the user. (Assuming they are listening with speakers or headphones, of course.)

It's really straightforward. So, click on the extension to add it to your project.

Now you have a new "Text to Speech" category in your list, with 3 new blocks available:

Text to Speech

speak hello

set voice to alto

set language to English

So, let's jump right in.

As always, when we are starting a new project, drag the "Events" block "When the green flag is clicked" into your editor.

Then connect a "speak" block to it, and set the message you want your program to speak:

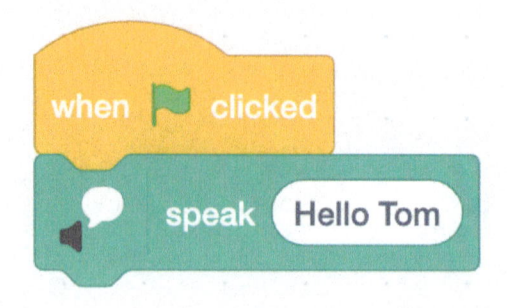

when ⚑ clicked
speak Hello Tom

So, click run - and you will hear "Hello Tom" or whatever your message is set to.

(If you don't hear anything, make sure that you have your volume turned up and your internet connection works. Sometimes, using a different browser also helps.)

See, the "speak" block works like any other Scratch block. It has a round shape, so you can have Scratch speak anything that has a round shape.

Here's your next exercise:

Let's ask the user for their name and then greet them personally.

Easy, right?

Here's what the program will look like:

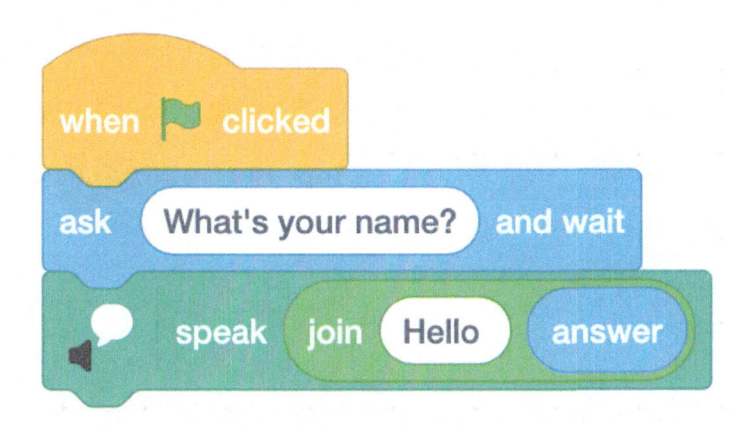

So, you see that using Scratch extensions is like using any other block. The form of the shapes will define what kind of blocks you can use inside these extension blocks.

Pretty cool, don't you think?

BUILD A TRANSLATOR

Let's try a different extension.

Click the blue button at the bottom again, and click the "Translate" extension.

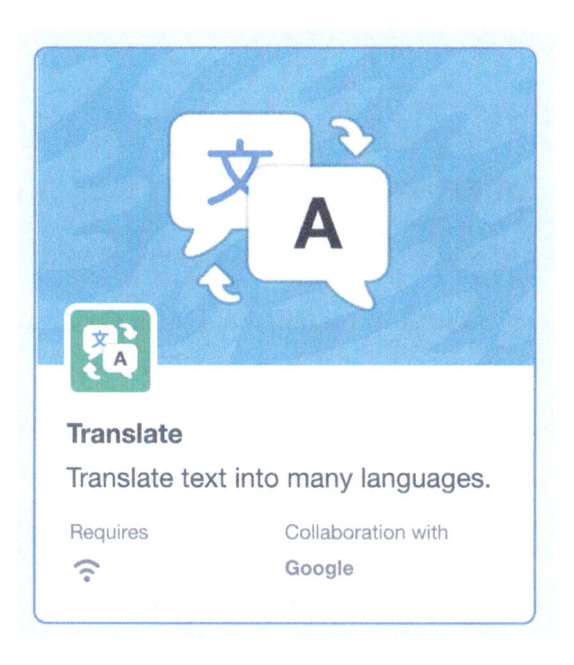

Translate
Translate text into many languages.

Requires 📶

Collaboration with Google

Let's use the "translate" block provided by this extension to translate a word that the user enters into another language:

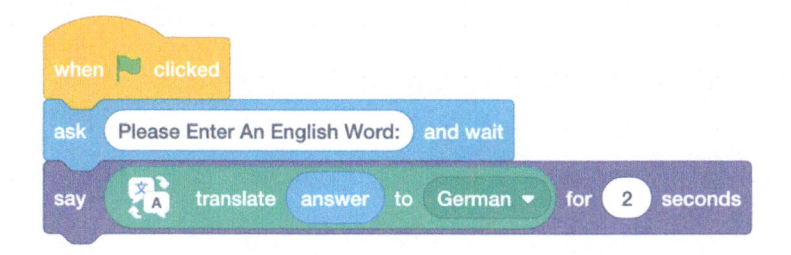

```
when [flag] clicked
ask (Please Enter An English Word:) and wait
say (translate (answer) to (German ▼)) for (2) seconds
```

155

Let's test that:

I enter "speed limit"

and I get back "Erlaubte Höchstgeschwindigkeit,"

which is another way to say one of my favorite German words:

"Geschwindigkeitsbegrenzung."

Play around with it.

Choose a different language to translate into.

Do you see how easy it is to use these extensions?

It's fun to experiment with lots of different functionality and interactivity that the various Scratch extensions provide.

Experiment, keep learning, keep making mistakes, keep learning from the mistakes.

That's the way to get better, to become an experienced programmer.

HOW TO LEARN ANY PROGRAMMING LANGUAGE

AREAS OF SOFTWARE DEVELOPMENT

Let's take it one step further and think about the future:

How can you apply the basic principles we have covered to learn another programming language?

We said that "programming" is thinking up instructions to give to a machine and transforming those ideas into a written language that the computer can understand.

In our case, the "language" that we used was Scratch. But there are many other programming languages used for different purposes.

And in this chapter, I want to show you how to take the principles that we learned with Scratch and apply them to any modern programming language.

There are too many programming languages to choose from. So the first question you should be asking yourself is: "What kind of programs do I want to create? What area of software development am I interested in?"

To help you answer that question, let me cover first what the different areas of software development are:

DIFFERENT AREAS

- Frontend Development
- Backend Development
- Mobile App Development
- Enterprise Systems
- Game Development
- Machine Learning, "Artificial Intelligence"
- Research

Frontend Development

The "frontend" of a particular software is everything facing the user, like a web page or a mobile app; the parts that are presented to the user and that they can interact with.

For example, if you order something on an eCommerce site like Amazon - the web pages that you see, the texts and images and the buttons you press to add something to your shopping cart, the order form you fill out - that's all frontend.

And as with all the other areas, certain programming languages are highly relevant for frontend development - and other ones that you would not typically use when you are doing frontend development work. (We will cover them shortly.)

Backend Development

The "backend" is everything the user does not see - like a database, any processing or calculations on a server, with no direct user interaction.

Again, thinking of an eCommerce site - the backend would be what needs to get done to actually fulfill your order. Communicating with the payment system, updating the inventory in the database, etc.

Mobile App Development

This particular area is still growing and changing massively - and we are all personally familiar with it, at least from the user's perspective.

App development usually involves many typical front-end tasks. Still, the technology and languages are different enough to think of "Mobile App Development" as its own area in software development.

Enterprise Systems

Enterprise systems are usually concerned with vast amounts of data, usually for big corporations, like insurance companies or banks.

Game Development

Game development is inherently different from many other areas - usually math-heavy, and performance considerations and optimizations matter a lot.

Machine Learning

Machine learning, sometimes called "artificial intelligence," is also a fascinating (relatively) new area where much progress is being made every year. It's also quite math-heavy and plays a significant role for companies who sit on a lot of data (again, institutions like insurance companies or banks).

Research

If you are a scientist and need to write custom programs to help with your research, there are specific languages there that would help you in your research tasks there.

What are the most essential languages in use right now?

We will talk about three major languages in greater detail:

- Python,
- JavaScript, and
- Java.

These are the top three languages right now, they've been there at the top three spots for the last couple of years, and it looks like this won't change much in the foreseeable future.

So, let's discuss how each language fits into the different areas that we talked about:

PYTHON

Programming Language Profile: Python

- ~~Frontend Development~~
- ~~Backend Development~~
- ~~Mobile App Development~~
- ~~Enterprise Systems~~
- ~~Game Development~~
- **Machine Learning**
- **Research**
- **Math**

Python is massive in the machine learning arena and very important for research.

If you're heavily into math, that's really where Python shines. It's a general-purpose language - that means you can do all the other stuff more or less. Still, it's not proprietary or attached to any system.

There are lots of frameworks and libraries available to extend its functionality. The language is easy to learn, and it definitely shines in the three areas: machine learning, research, and math.

JAVASCRIPT

Programming Language Profile: JavaScript

- **Frontend Development**
- **Backend Development**
- ~~Mobile App Development~~
- ~~Enterprise Systems~~
- ~~Game Development~~
- ~~Machine Learning~~
- ~~Research~~

JavaScript has a big community in front-end development - the overwhelming majority of websites are using JavaScript in one form or another.

JavaScript is the general-purpose language that makes websites interactive.

So if you are interested in front-end development, you should definitely think about learning JavaScript.

There are also backend frameworks like Node.js that use JavaScript (or its successor, TypeScript).

While you can use JavaScript (or JavaScript-like languages) to create mobile apps, it's not really big in that area.

You also see some JavaScript in machine learning - but it's not the most typical language to use in that field.

JAVA

Programming Language Profile: Java

- ~~Frontend Development~~
- **Backend Development**
- **Mobile App Development**
- **Enterprise Systems**
- ~~Game Development~~
- ~~Machine Learning~~
- ~~Research~~

Java is a universal programming language. It is cross-platform, meaning it has a powerful virtual machine that can run on different computers and devices, no matter what the platform is.

It is often used for back-end development in enterprise systems and for mobile apps - most Android apps are written in Java.

It is even possible to write games in Java - the original "Minecraft" which sold millions of copies worldwide, was written in Java. (Admittedly, it's not the typical language you would use to develop a game - but it shows the universal nature of Java.)

In my opinion, the best use case for Java is...

learning to program.

It's a modern object-oriented programming language, easy to understand, regularly updated, and expanded.

Last but not least, there are a lot of jobs available for Java developers - and this won't change in the future since lots of enterprise systems use Java.

How to Select YOUR Programming Language

So, which programming language should **you** learn?

As you probably have guessed, it depends on the direction you want to go and the area of software development that interests you the most.

But, if you are not sure, or if you are just getting started, I would recommend **Java**.

Not Sure?
Just Getting Started?

Why? The principles you learn in Java can be applied to many other languages. With the "curly-braces" syntax of Java, you really understand the basic structure of all these languages (and even a few more):

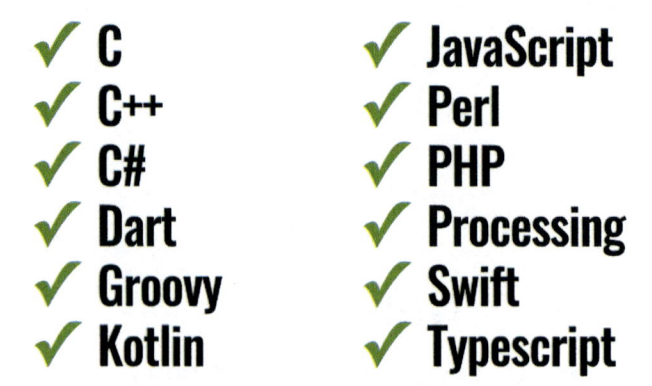

- ✓ C
- ✓ C++
- ✓ C#
- ✓ Dart
- ✓ Groovy
- ✓ Kotlin
- ✓ JavaScript
- ✓ Perl
- ✓ PHP
- ✓ Processing
- ✓ Swift
- ✓ Typescript

Compare that to Python - the syntax situation is really different.

Python has a more specific, unique syntax that's not really easily applicable to lots of other programming languages.

If you want to keep learning with me, I have a special offer for you in the last chapter.

HOW TO LEARN ANY PROGRAMMING LANGUAGE

Let's look at a Scratch example and learn how the same functionality would be written in Python, JavaScript, and Java.

Scratch

Let's take this simple example in Scratch - a loop counter, counting from 1 to 3.

You have seen this before. Just as a quick reminder, here's what we are doing:

- Setting a variable value to 0
- Defining a loop header with a loop condition
- In the loop body, incrementing the variable by 1
- and outputting the variable.

Python

Let's look at the "translation" of what this looks like in Python:

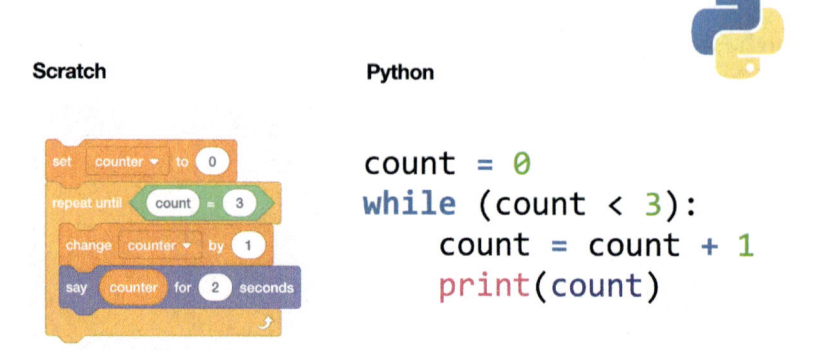

Scratch

Python

```
count = 0
while (count < 3):
    count = count + 1
    print(count)
```

Setting the counter variable to zero is equivalent to this line in Python:

`count = 0`

The variable is called "count".

The equal sign = means "set the value to the one on the right," and on the right-hand side is just a 0.

(The variable name I chose in the other language is "count" instead of Scratch's "counter" so that we can distinguish the two - but the variable name is not relevant.)

See? Nothing to be scared of!

Next on the left side, with Scratch:

repeat until "count" = 3.

We don't have the exact same loop type in Python, but we've got a "while" loop. It consists of the keyword "while", followed by the loop condition in parentheses:

```
while (count < 3 ):
```

The program will execute the loop body (that follows) repeatedly "while" (as long as) the value of "count" is less than 3.

The loop condition's logic is turned around:

In Scratch, the loop condition is considered the "stop" condition.

In Python, the loop condition is considered the "continue" condition.

Or, to put it in other words:

Scratch: Continue the loop **until** the given condition is **true**

Python: Continue the loop **while** the given condition is **true** (stop when the condition becomes false)

But if you think about it, it really is the same behavior, just two different ways to describe it:

In Scratch, we loop until the counter has reached 3.

In Python, we loop while (as long as) count has not yet reached 3.

Next is incrementing the "count" variable by 1. In Python, it's:

```
count = count + 1
```

Again, we've got the equal sign = here, the assignment operator.

The right-hand side of this assignment will be evaluated first.

So, on the right-hand side, the current value of "count" is taken, which is 0 after the start,

then 1 is added, so 0+1 equals 1.

Then the result of that calculation (1) is assigned to the left-hand side. So effectively, the "count" variable (that was 0) gets overwritten with the new value (1).

And what's important is that this line is indented - it doesn't start directly below the "while" line but is indented to the right.

Indented lines are essential in Python; they signal which lines belong to a code block (like the loop body, an if-then block, or something similar.)

```
while (count < 3):
    count = count + 1
```

Finally, the last block in the loop body in Scratch is "say counter for 2 seconds".

There are different ways to output stuff - the simplest option in Python is to use the "print" command:

```
print(count)
```

We have the parentheses ( ) here, they are equivalent to the round shapes in Scratch. Inside is the parameter that the "print" command takes. Everything between these two parentheses is being outputted to the screen (called the "console").

And note that this line is indented because it belongs to the loop body, too.

And that's it for Python.

JavaScript

Scratch

JavaScript

```javascript
var count = 0;
while (count < 3) {
    count = count + 1;
    console.log(count);
}
```

Next, let's see what JavaScript looks like in comparison.

You see some similarities to Python - but a few significant differences.

To declare and initialize the count variable, we have this line:

```
var count = 0;
```

Also, before using a variable for the first time, we need to declare it by writing "var" in front of it. It's the same as clicking the "Make a Variable" button in Scratch.

Note the semicolon at the end, which signals "this is the end of this statement."

Next, the while loop.

```
while (count < 3) {
```

It looks very familiar, but there's an opening curly brace at the end.

In JavaScript, curly braces indicate the beginning and the end of a code block - statements that belong together, like the body of a loop:

```
{

    ...

}
```

Remember that in Python, we used indention to indicate which statements belong to the loop body.

With JavaScript (and Java and other modern "C-style" programming languages), you need the opening and closing curly braces. You usually indent the lines between the curly braces as well, but it's purely for aesthetical reasons (to make it easier to identify the loop body at a glance - it's not required by the language).

Within the loop body, the first line is the same as in Python, again with a semicolon at the end of the line:

```
count = count + 1;
```

This increments the value of "count" by 1.

And then instead of "print," in Python, we've got this:

```
console.log(count);
```

That's the simplest command in JavaScript to print something out on the screen (again, called the "console").

Inside the parentheses ( ) is what we want to print out - in our case, the value of the variable "count."

And then we've got the closing curly brace here to indicate the end of the loop body:

```
}
```

Again - do you see how easy it is to relate what we've learned in Scratch to another language?

Variable assignments, loops, incrementing a value, outputting stuff - it's all there.

Java

Scratch **Java**

```java
int count = 0;
while (count < 3) {
    count = count + 1;
    System.out.println(count);
}
```

Let's continue our journey with the third of the three most important programming languages - Java.

Note: Although they have a similar name, JavaScript and Java are actually two completely different languages.

But as they are both "curly-braces" syntax languages, the statements look very similar, indeed.

We need to declare a variable before we can use it. But instead of "var count" as in JavaScript, we've got this:

```
int count = 0;
```

Java is a "strongly-typed" language, meaning we distinguish between different types of variables.

We have numerical types like "int" - they can only store integer (whole) numbers. Or the so-called "String" variables that can store text. And a few other types.

But other than that, it's really the same as before:

"count" is the variable name,

= is the assignment operator,

0 is the value.

And the semicolon at the end - same as with JavaScript.

The while statement and the increment statement are the same as in JavaScript:

```
while (count < 3) {
    count = count + 1;
```

We need the curly braces to indicate the loop body's start and end (again, the indention is optional).

Finally, instead of "console.log" in JavaScript or "print" in Python, in Java we have this:

```
    System.out.println(count);
}
```

println means "print line". The thing we want to output (the parameter to the println method) is inside the parentheses. We end the loop with the curly braces }.

Take a few more moments to compare these three languages with each other.

Of course, there are differences, particularly with Python - it doesn't have the curly braces; you need to indent the lines to indicate the loop body.

Java and JavaScript, on the other end, have very similar syntax.

YOUR NEXT STEP?

Congratulations!

You made it through the complete book! How do you feel?

I hope I could dispel some of the programming myths that programming is so difficult or complex or that you need to understand math...

I hope you realize now that none of that is actually true.

If you really break things down, take it step by step, learn the underlying principles and relate each topic to examples and concepts in the real world - it's actually quite easy.

So, what's next?

Let's fast forward a little bit into the future.

How about learning how to write real code in a modern programming language?

So you can start a new career,

get a promotion,

or develop real software programs, like mobile apps - and publish them to the world!

I will make you a special offer that is NOT for everyone.

I'm only making it available to you because you proved you're an action taker.

Here's the deal: I have a program called...

The "30 Day Java Challenge"

It's **the perfect next step for you** after working through this book.

Let me explain to you what the "30 Day Java Challenge" is and how it will help you:

We learn Java together from the ground up.

We already talked about Java being the top universal programming language used by millions of professional programmers today, ranging from enterprise software (for big companies like banks and insurances) to mobile apps for Android phones.

Even games like Minecraft - they all use Java.

So it's really a _universal_ programming language.

And in this course, in the 30 Day Java Challenge, we are GETTING IT DONE.

You will have a complete understanding of programming with Java. You will have written, executed, and tested your own Java programs.

And you will know where to head next.

How does it work exactly?

Every day for 30 days, you will receive a **new training video** from me, giving you crystal-clear explanations about the Java topic of the day.

Every day, you will also be given **an interactive online workbook** with the exact step-by-step instructions you need to follow to practice the topic for this day.

There is nothing to install to use the workbooks - you just need a web browser.

Now, when you are going through the training, what if you have any questions?

Throughout the challenge, we'll be **meeting each week**, personally, for a **live group call.**

So if you are stuck or have any remaining questions, I got you covered.

And if you miss a call, you can find the **call recordings** in a private membership group, specifically for this challenge, for more support and accountability from me and your fellow challengers.

And that's just the tip of the iceberg of what you'll get with the "30 Day Java Challenge"!

I cannot list all the great bonuses you will get for free when joining me in the "30 Day Java Challenge" here.

But let me point out one specific bonus:

We all know that practice makes perfect, right?

Well, with the 30 Day Java Challenge, you will get access **to 101 Interactive Java Coding Exercises and Solution Video**s from me personally.

I'm walking you step by step through each exercise, with clear explanations of how to solve each. If there's more than one way to solve an exercise, we also cover all the alternatives.

Each solution video is between 5 and 30 minutes long, and you get 101 (in words: one hundred and one) of them.

So, you can see that even after you have finished the challenge, you will have plenty of ways to practice every day.

So, here's the thing.

You don't even need to think about it right now.

Just enroll in the challenge, take the complete course, ask me questions and participate in the group calls - and if you don't love it, for any reason, just email me within **30 day**s for a **full money-back guarantee**.

You have just completed the "Programming Secrets" System.

Don't miss your chance for the next step - to learn and master a real, essential programming language.

With your dedication and my help and motivation as your mentor in the "30 Day Java Challenge", you can learn programming in a modern language faster and easier than ever.

Your Next Step?

Type in this address to get started:

teachmetom.com/no-code-java

THANK YOU!

If you received value from this book, then I'd like to ask you for a favor: Would you be kind enough to leave a review for this book on Amazon?

⭐ ⭐ ⭐ ⭐ ⭐

It really helps.

Thanks!

Your Mentor
Tom

ABOUT THE AUTHOR

Tom Schweitzer is the founder of TeachMeTom.

He is focused on leveraging his decades-long experience as a software industry professional to teach students worldwide.

Tom has worked for major companies like IBM, Alcatel, Rockstar Games and VeriSign.

He also co-founded numerous startups and published his own mobile apps with over 2.5 million organic downloads.

Tom has taught various topics, from project management, programming, Java, JavaScript, HTML, agile principles, Scrum, to mobile app development, and other software development topics.

He is a licensed Scrum Master and Scrum Project Owner.

Tom works and lives with his family in Vienna, Austria. He enjoys sailing, playing keyboards in his band, and going to the many theaters in Vienna.

To learn more about Tom's courses, go to teachmetom.com

Printed in Great Britain
by Amazon